Competition and Cooperative Bargaining Models in Supply Chains

Competition and Cooperative Bargaining Models in Supply Chains

Fernando Bernstein

Duke University
Durham, NC 27708-0120
USA
fernando@duke.edu

Mahesh Nagarajan

University of British Columbia
Vancouver, BC
Canada
mahesh.nagarajan@sauder.ubc.ca

the essence of knowledge

Boston – Delft

Foundations and Trends® in Technology, Information and Operations Management

Published, sold and distributed by:
now Publishers Inc.
PO Box 1024
Hanover, MA 02339
USA
Tel. +1-781-985-4510
www.nowpublishers.com
sales@nowpublishers.com

Outside North America:
now Publishers Inc.
PO Box 179
2600 AD Delft
The Netherlands
Tel. +31-6-51115274

The preferred citation for this publication is F. Bernstein and M. Nagarajan, Competition and Cooperative Bargaining Models in Supply Chains, Foundation and Trends® in Technology, Information and Operations Management, vol 5, no 2, pp 87–145, 2011

ISBN: 978-1-60198-556-9
© 2012 F. Bernstein and M. Nagarajan

Foundations and Trends® in Technology, Information and Operations Management

Volume 5 Issue 2, 2011

Editorial Board

Editorial Scope

Foundations and Trends® in Technology, Information and Operations Management will publish survey and tutorial articles in the following topics:

- B2B Commerce
- Business Process Engineering and Design
- Business Process Outsourcing
- Capacity Planning
- Competitive Operations
- Contracting in Supply Chains
- E-Commerce and E-Business Models
- Electronic markets, auctions and exchanges
- Enterprise Management Systems
- Facility Location
- Information Chain Structure and Competition
- International Operations
- Marketing/Manufacturing Interfaces
- Multi-location inventory theory

- New Product & Service Design
- Queuing Networks
- Reverse Logistics
- Service Logistics and Product Support
- Supply Chain Management
- Technology Management and Strategy
- Technology, Information and Operations in:
  - Automotive Industries
  - Electronics manufacturing
  - Financial Services
  - Health Care
  - Industrial Equipment
  - Media and Entertainment
  - Process Industries
  - Retailing
  - Telecommunications

Information for Librarians

Foundations and Trends® in Technology, Information and Operations Management, 2011, Volume 5, 4 issues. ISSN paper version 1571-9545. ISSN online version 1571-9553. Also available as a combined paper and online subscription.

Foundations and Trends® in
Technology, Information and Operations Management
Vol. 5, No. 2 (2011) 87–145
© 2012 F. Bernstein and M. Nagarajan
DOI: 10.1561/0200000016

the essence of knowledge

Competition and Cooperative Bargaining Models in Supply Chains

Fernando Bernstein[1] and Mahesh Nagarajan[2]

[1] The Fuqua School of Business, Duke University, Durham, NC
27708-0120, USA, fernando@duke.edu
[2] Sauder School of Business, University of British Columbia, Vancouver,
BC, Canada, mahesh.nagarajan@sauder.ubc.ca

Abstract

In the last two decades or so, a significant emphasis of the research
literature in operations management has been on the strategic interaction of firms in a supply chain. Individual firms in supply chains make
decisions on multiple levers such as capacity, inventory and price, to
name a few, that have consequences for the entire supply chain. In modeling strategic interactions, the operations literature has followed the
large literature in industrial organization and economics. Competition
between firms in a supply chain has largely been modeled using non-
cooperative game theory and the associated concepts of equilibrium
that predict the outcomes. There are a few key differences between
the industrial organization literature and the research in operations
management. First of all, the operations literature looks more at operational variables, such as capacity and inventory, as a response to various sources of process uncertainty that any firm faces. The preferences
of individual customers, their valuations and the construction of the
specific form of the uncertainty is less of a concern (although more

recent literature emphasize this). Second, the findings in the operations literature usually have the objective of improving individual firms' (and supply chains') profits and operational efficiencies rather than one of dictating economic policy. Third, although non-cooperative models are the norm, there is also an underlying emphasis in the operations literature on cooperation between firms in a supply chain to improve the overall profit of the supply chain. This is probably because, unlike the levers traditionally studied in economics, many operational variables in a supply chain are often jointly decided between firms. The goal of this review taps on this last sentiment. We provide an overview of some of the basic multi-firm models studied in supply chain management. We look at how the literature uses non-cooperative game theory to analyze these models. We then look at how some of these models can be analyzed using a cooperative bargaining framework. We compare the modeling tools and the insights one obtains by taking this twofold approach. This process also allows us to discuss a few topics of interest such as the relative channel power of a firm, the relative merits of using a non-cooperative game versus cooperative bargaining to model a supply chain setting, etc. Finally, we conclude this review by exploring some issues that remain unresolved and are topics for future research.

Contents

1

Modeling and Analyzing Competition

1.1 Introduction

Supply chains often consist of several tiers or echelons, each with one or more firms. In a decentralized multi-tier supply chain, materials (components, products) flow through the system across multiple independent firms until they reach the end-customer. In this process, firms invest in effort (innovation, product development, quality, etc.), build manufacturing capacity, assemble components, store products, and set prices, all of which require managerial decisions which are generally based on each firm's self-serving interest. The structure of supply chains can vary substantially. Some industries are characterized by multiple suppliers producing components that are assembled by a relatively small number of final assemblers, while in others the opposite occurs. Likewise, there is a relatively small number of manufacturers producing consumer goods, but a large number of retailers selling those products to the market. Some of these retailers compete directly in the downstream market, while others are local monopolists. Papers analyzing competition in supply chains restrict attention to a certain portion of the system (e.g., one manufacturer and one retailer, one manufacturer and multiple retailers, multiple suppliers and one buyer or assembler,

1

etc.). Competition in supply chains arises across firms in the same tier (horizontal competition), across firms in different tiers (vertical competition), or both.

In settings with horizontal competition, firms typically make their decisions simultaneously. Their equilibrium decisions are determined by the Nash equilibrium concept [80]. In the OM literature, horizontal competition generally involves competition through inventory availability, innovation or sales effort, quality, products' prices, warranties, or other dimensions of customer service, across firms in the same tier. For example, if a firm lowers its price (or increases inventory availability, sales effort, or its service level), the demand experienced by its competitors is likely to decrease. Vertical interactions are generally governed by one or more leading firms that move first by offering a contract — a natural strategy of interaction between parties — to other firms in the supply chain network. The contract may be as simple as a wholesale price contract. Other commonly studied contracts involve buy-back policies, revenue sharing agreements, quantity discounts, two-part tariffs, vertical price restraints, etc. (We will discuss many of these contracts later in the review.) The sequential timing of decisions leads to a Stackelberg game [59]. The leader makes its decision in anticipation of the decisions made by the followers. The contract sequence is one of the factors that may determine the relative power of firms in the supply chain. We discuss this issue later in this section. Some models in the supply-chain management literature consider a combination of vertical and horizontal competition. For example, a set of competing firms buys a product from a common upstream supplier (manufacturer) or sells complementary products to an assembler. This section reviews a representative set of papers in operations management addressing models of vertical and/or horizontal competition, particularly focused on capacity, inventory, and price competition. The scope of the review is limited to those models of competition as we have counterpart work examining the role of negotiation and cooperative bargaining in such models.

In decentralized supply chains, firms make decisions to optimize their own cost or profit, ignoring the implications of their actions on other firms in the system. That is, firms do not internalize the cost or benefit implied by their decisions. A challenge encountered in these systems consists of structuring the costs and rewards of all the firms to align their objectives with the aggregate supply-chain wide profit — namely, achieve supply-chain coordination. Supply-chain coordination requires modification of firms' incentives. This can be accomplished with contractual arrangements between the parties in the supply chain that allow individual firms to internalize the externalities imposed by their actions on other firms. A vast literature in operations management explores the design and practical applicability of coordinating contracts. This manuscript does not intend to provide a comprehensive review of the literature on supply-chain coordination. We refer the reader to Anupindi and Bassok [4, 5], Lariviere [62], Corbett and Tang [38], Cachon [20], and Li and Wang [66] for reviews on this subject.

We begin this section with a description of what we call the atomic model — one with a single manufacturer or supplier selling to a single retailer. We then consider settings with multiple firms in either the downstream or upstream tier of the supply chain — a distribution and an assembly system, respectively. This is followed by a review of models of competition in more complex supply chain networks and by a discussion of the role of Stackelberg leadership in modeling the firms' relative power in a supply chain.

1.2 The Atomic Model

Let us first look at a setting with vertical competition between a manufacturer selling to a single retailer, as illustrated in Figure 1.1.

A significant set of papers in operations management look at models with exogenous prices to isolate the effects of uncertainty and related inventory decisions. In practice, this applies to a class of products where a retailer has little wiggle room on retail prices, perhaps due to competition. In such settings, the manufacturer sets the terms of the contract (e.g., a wholesale price), based on which the retailer determines a stocking level. Demand is uncertain, so the retailer's purchasing decision involves the solution of a newsvendor problem.

The paper by Lariviere and Porteus [64] focuses on the interaction between a manufacturer and a newsvendor-type retailer in a market with stochastic demand and exogenous retail price. Using

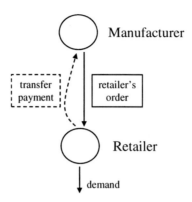

Fig. 1.1 Atomic model.

the Stackelberg framework, the paper examines the efficiency of the decentralized supply chain (as measured by the performance of the decentralized system relative to the centralized optimal profit) and the division of supply chain profit. Demand is assumed to follow a continuous distribution Φ with density ϕ. The manufacturer's marginal production cost is c and the fixed selling price is $r > c$. In the integrated system, the joint profit of the manufacturer and the retailer, as a function of the stocking level y, is given by $\Pi^I(y) = -cy + r\int_0^y \xi\phi(\xi)d\xi + ry(1 - \Phi(y))$. This function is concave in y, with maximizer $y^I = \Phi^{-1}[(r - c)/r]$. Under decentralized control, the retailer faces a similar problem as in the integrated system, but with the wholesale price $w > c$ replacing the production cost c. The retailer's optimal order quantity is $y(w) = \Phi^{-1}[(r - w)/r] < y^I$ — this strictly lower-than-system-optimal order quantity indicates a loss of efficiency due to decentralization. As the Stackelberg leader, the manufacturer chooses the wholesale price to maximize $\Pi^M(w) = (w - c)y(w)$. Since there is a one-to-one correspondence between wholesale price and stocking quantity, the manufacturer equivalently chooses a stocking quantity y to maximize $\Pi^M(y) = w(y)y - cy$, where $w(y) = r(1 - \Phi(y))$. To solve the Stackelberg game, the paper identifies a condition on the stochastic demand function that guarantees the unimodality of the manufacturer's profit. Specifically, the requirement is that the demand distribution belong to the class of distributions with an increasing generalized failure rate, that is, that the generalized failure rate of the distribution Φ, defined as $g(\xi) = \xi\phi(\xi)/(1 - \Phi(\xi))$, be an increasing function of ξ (refer to Lariviere [63] for more details). This finding implies that the optimal retailer stocking quantity in the decentralized system (that itself determines the optimal wholesale price charged by the manufacturer) is the solution to the manufacturer's first-order condition $(1 - \Phi(y))(1 - g(y)) = c/r$. The function $\nu(y) = 1/g(y)$ measures the elasticity of the retailer's order at the stocking level y, that is, the change in the retailer's order from a percent increase (or decrease) in the wholesale price. At the optimal manufacturer wholesale price w^*, both the manufacturer and the retailer earn positive margins $w^* - c$ and $r - w^*$, respectively. This is the "double marginalization" effect [103] that leads to system inefficiency — that is, the total profit in the decentralized system is less than that in the centralized system. A wholesale price higher than marginal cost leads to a lower retailer stocking quantity as compared to the optimal stocking quantity in the centralized system. In this atomic model, even though there are essentially two players differentiated only by their role, we see competition between these two players as they both compete on the margins they make from sales.

A buy-back contract (or returns policy) coordinates the supply chain composed of a single manufacturer selling to a newsvendor, provided that the retail price is exogenous. Under a returns policy, the manufacturer buys all unsold inventory back from the retailer at a given buy-back rate. That is, the wholesale price w is supplemented with a buy-back rate $b < w$ paid by the manufacturer to the retailer at the end of the selling season for all units unsold. Under a returns policy, the retailer's expected profit is given by $\Pi^R(y) = -wy + r \int_0^y \xi\phi(\xi)d\xi + ry(1 - \Phi(y)) + b(y - \int_0^y \xi\phi(\xi)d\xi)$, where the last term represents manufacturer payments for unsold products. The optimal stocking quantity for the retailer is $y(w, b) = \Phi^{-1}[(r - w)/(r - b)]$. As shown in Pasternack [89], an appropriately designed buy-back contract coordinates the supply chain. Moreover, this contract allows for an arbitrary division of the supply-chain profit. A returns policy offers the retailer an incentive to order more by essentially transferring some of the risk associated with demand uncertainty to the manufacturer. See Kandel [56] and Emmons and Gilbert [42] for additional discussion on returns policies.

In the spirit of a returns policy, supply chain coordination in the atomic model can be achieved through a quantity flexibility contract. Under this contract, the newsvendor retailer places an order y with the manufacturer, who commits to providing $y(1 + u)$ units to the retailer, with $u \leq 0$. Once demand is realized, the retailer commits to ordering at least $y(1 - d)$ units from the manufacturer, with $0 \leq d < 1$. That is, instead of returning unsold units at the end of the selling season, the retailer can cancel a portion of its initial order if demand is low. Taylor [105] shows that, in a supply chain consisting of a manufacturer selling to a single newsvendor retailer, channel coordination can also be achieved with a rebate contract. This contract specifies a payment to the retailer (rebate) for each unit sold beyond a pre-determined target.

When prices are endogenous, the newsvendor retailer selects both a stocking quantity y and a retail price p. Demand is a function of the retail price and is assumed to be of the multiplicative form, i.e., $D(p, \epsilon) = d(p)\epsilon$, or of the additive form, i.e., $D(p, \epsilon) = d(p) + \epsilon$, where $d(p)$ is a deterministic downward sloping function of price and ϵ is a random term, independent of p. (Petruzzi and Dada [91] provide a comprehensive review of results regarding the optimal decisions of a price-setting newsvendor.) Bernstein and Federgruen [14] show that no buy-back contract is capable of coordinating a decentralized system with a price-setting newsvendor, except for a trivial contract in which the wholesale price equals marginal cost and the buy-back rate is set to zero (if the retailer has a positive salvage value, then the buy-back rate must equal the retailer's salvage value). Song et al. [102] examine structural properties of buy-back contracts in a decentralized system with a manufacturer selling to a price-setting newsvendor. The paper considers a Stacklberg setting, with the manufacturer as the leader. Under the assumption of an increasing generalized failure rate, as in Larivere and Porteus [64], and under an assumption on the curvature of $d(p)$, the paper shows that the retailer's stocking and pricing problem has a unique solution. The assumption on $d(p)$ requires that the elasticity $\eta(p) = -p(d'(p)/d(p))$ be increasing in p, $p/\eta(p)$ be monotone and convex, and $p(1 - 1/\eta(p))$ be strictly increasing in p. The assumptions on $d(p)$ guarantee that the retailer's profit is unimodal in p and, together with the increasing generalized failure rate assumption on the distribution of the random term, imply that the retailer's pricing and stocking problem under a given buy-back contract has a unique solution. This enables the authors to derive properties of the manufacturer's profit function and, in turn, characterize the optimal contract parameters. Moreover, the paper identifies conditions on $d(p)$ under which the optimal manufacturer buy-back contract is independent of the demand distribution. Refer to Granot and Yin [49] and Liu et al. [68] for related studies of decentralized supply chains with endogenous price-dependent demand — the former under buy-back contracts and the latter under an ex-ante retailer commitment to a fixed retail price markup.

Revenue-sharing contracts supplement a unit wholesale price with transfer payments that comprise a percentage of the revenues $0 \leq \alpha \leq 1$ generated in the supply chain. These contracts are common, for example, in the video-rental industry. Similar pay-on-production contracts are prevalent in the automobile industry. Cachon and Lariviere [23] study revenue-sharing contracts in supply chains with a supplier selling to one or multiple competing retailers (or any link between two levels in the supply chain). Retailer revenues are determined by its purchase quantities and selling price. The model is quite general, allowing for deterministic or stochastic demand. In a setting with a single retailer, a revenue-sharing contract coordinates the supply chain and the system profit can be arbitrarily divided among firms. In fact, in that setting, a revenue-sharing contract is equivalent to a buy-back contract. A revenue-sharing contract also coordinates a supply chain consisting of competing retailers with exogenously determined prices. Consider a system with n retailers. Let $R_i(q)$ denote the expected revenue of retailer i associated with a vector of stocking levels $q = (q_1, \ldots, q_n)$. $R_i(q)$ is assumed to be decreasing in q_i and $\partial^2 R_i / \partial q_i \partial q_j \leq 0$, that is, inventory at different retailers are substitutes. Letting c_i denote the system's cost associated with producing and selling products to retailer i, the total supply chain profit is $\sum_{i=1}^{n} (R_i(q) - c_i q_i)$. The revenue-sharing contract consists of a wholesale-price w_i, revenue-share α_i pair for each retailer i. The coordinating revenue-sharing contract includes a term that reflects the externalities each retailer imposes on its competitors. In the atomic model, the parameter α in a revenue-sharing contract serves the purpose of allocating the profits between the supplier and the retailer. Cachon and Lariviere [23] state that, "The particular profit split chosen probably depends on the firms' relative bargaining power. As the retailer's bargaining position becomes stronger, one would anticipate [α] increases. As a proxy for bargaining power, each firm may have an outside opportunity profit... that the firm requires to engage in the relationship."

As indicated, many of the contracts discussed earlier allow for an arbitrary division of the supply chain profit between the manufacturer and the retailer (through the appropriate choice of the contract parameters). In some cases, the terms of the contract are specified a priori by the manufacturer and remain unmovable. In others, the contract adopted in the supply chain is the result of a negotiation process between the parties. This aspect of the contract negotiation is generally ignored in much of the literature that analyzes competition using a non-cooperative game approach. In the next section, we present a cooperative bargaining framework to explore the process of contract negotiation.

A number of papers explore vertical competition in infinite horizon, decentralized supply-chain settings. Cachon and Zipkin [26] study a two-stage decentralized series system. Both firms in the serial system share a portion of the penalties incurred for consumer backorders and independently select the base-stock levels to minimize their own costs. The paper analyzes two games that differ in how firms track their inventory levels — the echelon game, in which firms follow echelon policies (a firm's echelon inventory is its local inventory plus all inventory downstream in the supply chain), and the local game, in which they use local policies — and compares the resulting equilibria. Cachon [21] considers a two-echelon supply chain with one supplier and multiple retailers in which all firms operate under a continuous review inventory policy. All retailers are identical. The supplier's policy parameters impact the retailers' cost functions (e.g., a late retailer shipment may lead to retail backorders), and vice versa. The game between the supplier and the retailers is supermodular, that is, the action set of each firm is a compact lattice and the marginal change in a firm's cost due to an increase in one of its action variables is increasing in any other of its competitors' action variables. The paper shows that, in some settings, the optimal policy in the centralized system arises as a Nash equilibrium. Unlike the papers described earlier, the above models assume away any leadership position induced by the role of the Stackelberg leader and analyze simultaneous competition between the upstream and downstream firms. (Cachon and Zipkin show that endowing one player with Stackelberg leadership in general changes the equilibrium base-stock levels relative to a setting with simultaneous competition.)

In most existing infinite-horizon models of competition in the operations management literature, decisions are made at the beginning of the season once and for all, reducing the complexity involved in modeling the firms' interactions over time. In multi-period settings, decisions made in each period use information from the history of transactions up to that point and anticipate the other firms' reactions to this period's decisions in future periods. These so-called closed-loop games are significantly more complex as the firms' equilibrium decisions need to contemplate the future repercussions of their current actions. Very little work has been done in this area so far, so this remains a research topic of relevance that is worth pursuing. Nevertheless, there has recently been greater interest in multi-period games that explicitly model operational interactions. Parker and Kapuscinski [87] consider a decentralized two-stage serial supply chain with capacity limits. By appropriately setting the salvage value functions, the paper inductively shows that the cost function in each period is separable in a certain domain, in a way that helps ensure the existence of a closed-loop, subgame perfect equilibrium. The equilibrium policy is a modified echelon base-stock policy. The paper also examines the performance of the decentralized system relative to the first-best solution and discusses the need for a coordinating contract.

1.3 Two-Stage Systems with Retailer Competition

In a system with a single manufacturer and a single retailer, supply-chain coordination can also be achieved by using a two-part tariff that involves a wholesale price equal to the production cost and a side payment given by a fixed fee. The manufacturer can collect all profits

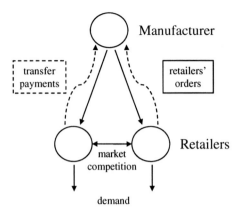

Fig. 1.2 Retailer competition.

through the fixed fee. Therefore, the incentive problem discussed above has a fairly simple remedy. In contrast, in a system with a manufacturer selling to two competing retailers, Krishnan and Winter [60] discuss the presence of two externalities that distort the firms' decisions. Figure 1.2 illustrates this setting.

The vertical externality arises because, as the retail price is increased, the manufacturer collects the wholesale mark-up on a lower quantity sold through the retailer. The horizontal externality arises through the cross-price elasticity of demand between the two retailers. The authors find that a two-part tariff alone cannot coordinate this system — it needs to be complemented with a vertical price floor that restricts the range of retail prices available to the retailers (i.e., a lower bound on the price the retailer can charge). The system can also be coordinated with a wholesale price combined with a buy-back contract and a fixed fee. The paper then considers a system with two competing retailers making pricing and inventory decisions, in which excess demand at one retailer spills over to the other retailer. The coordinating contract is significantly more complex in that setting, and may again require a price floor on the retail price.

Horizontal competition plays a central role in supply-chain settings in which retailers compete in the downstream market. Supermodular games naturally arise in many models of horizontal competition — in those models, the firms' decisions are strategic complements, that is, the increase in a firm's own decision (e.g., its price) leads to an increase in the marginal change of its competitors' payoffs with respect to their own decisions (in that example, their own prices). Bernstein and Federgruen [12] consider a distribution system in which one supplier sells products to multiple competing retailers. The supplier and each retailer i incur inventory-carrying costs h_0 and h_i, respectively, while all supplier orders and transfers to retailer i incur fixed costs K_0 and K_i, respectively, and variable costs c_0 and c_i, respectively. All firms make decisions regarding their selling prices and replenishment strategies. Market demand is deterministic and retailers engage in either price or quantity competition. Under price competition, demand at each retailer i is a function of all retailer prices, $d_i(p)$, which is decreasing in retailer i's own price and increasing in the competitors' prices. The paper analyzes the decentralized system, in which the supplier acts as the Stackelberg leader setting wholesale prices and the retailers follow by choosing their policy variables. Specifically, retailer i follows a power-of-two policy with replenishment interval T_i (under a power-of-two policy, the retailer gets replenished when its inventory level is down to zero and replenishments arrive after a constant interval, which is chosen as a power-of-two multiple of a base period) and sets a price p_i. Retailer i's profit function is given by $\pi_i(p_i, T_i | p_{-i}, w_i) = (p_i - c_i - w_i)d_i(p) - \frac{K_i}{T_i} - \frac{1}{2}d_i(p)h_iT_i$ and it is a function of the retailer's own decision variables, the wholesale price w_i, and the vector of prices of retailer i's competitors, p_{-i}. Existence and uniqueness of a Nash equilibrium requires a condition that relates each retailer's demand price elasticity with the ratio of its annual sales to its combined inventory and fixed setup costs: $\epsilon_{ii} \leq \frac{4 \times \text{REV}_i}{\text{INV}_i}$, where $\epsilon_{ii} = -\frac{\partial d_i(p)}{\partial p_i}\frac{p_i}{d_i(p)}$ is retailer i's price elasticity, $\text{REV}_i = p_i d_i(p)$ is retailer i's total gross revenue, and $\text{INV}_i = \sqrt{2d_i(p)h_iK_i}$ is retailer i's optimal total inventory and setup cost. Under this condition, the paper shows that the retailer game is supermodular and has a unique Nash equilibrium. The paper provides empirical evidence to demonstrate that this condition is generally satisfied in practice. The paper concludes with a discussion of a coordinating contract that involves a quantity discount as well as a discount based on each retailer's order frequency. (Several papers examine the effectiveness of quantity discounts in distribution channels, see, e.g., Weng [112, 111], Munson and Rosenblatt [76], Corbett and de Groote [36], Chen et al. [31], Viswanathan and Wang [107], and Altintas et al. [3].)

With a focus on horizontal competition, Bernstein and Federgruen [13] study a model of multiple retailers facing stochastic demands and competing in terms of their retail prices and service levels. Retailers operate following a periodic review, infinite-horizon inventory policy. The paper considers three settings that differ in the sequence in which retailers make decisions. In the first setting, firms engage in price competition while their service levels are exogenously set. In the second setting, firms simultaneously choose a service level and a combined price and inventory strategy. In the last setting, firms make their decisions sequentially, first selecting a service level and subsequently choosing a combined pricing and inventory strategy with full knowledge of the service levels selected by all competitors. The conclusion is that, in general, the equilibrium service level in the two-stage game may differ significantly from the one arising in the simultaneous game. However, under certain demand specifications, each firm adopts the same equilibrium service level in both settings. This further illustrates how the order of play may impact the firms' equilibrium decisions and the resulting division of supply-chain profit. Bernstein and Federgruen [14] study the equilibrium behavior of a set of competing retailers in a newsvendor setting. Prices are endogenous, but unsatisfied demand at a store is lost. Retailers make simultaneous ordering and pricing decisions. The paper provides conditions that ensure that the retailer game has a unique Nash equilibrium. Supply-chain coordination in this setting requires a non-linear price-discount sharing scheme, under which the supplier subsidizes a portion of the retailers' retail price discounts. Bernstein and Federgruen [15] and Krishnan and Winter [61] explore retailer competition and supply-chain coordination in multi-period settings. In a supply chain consisting of a manufacturer selling to two competing retailers, Kostamis and Ziya [58] examine the role of retailer cost asymmetry and competition intensity on the manufacturer's optimal contract.

Several papers explore models of inventory-based competition. One of the earliest papers on this subject is Parlar [88]. Anupindi and Bassok [4, 5] considers a manufacturer selling a product to two retailers that compete in the downstream market. Specifically, a fraction of customers that find the product out of stock in one location, visit the second retailer to look for the product there. The retailers can maintain the stocks in their own locations, or pool inventory at a central location. The paper shows that centralization may not benefit the manufacturer. Rather, retailer competition may lead to higher aggregate sales than centralization, resulting in greater benefit to the manufacturer. Mahajan and Van Ryzin [70] analyze inventory competition between multiple retailers in a newsvendor setting. Customers choose where to buy a product based on the retailers' product availability. Demand at each retail store is stochastically decreasing in the other retailers' stocking levels. Based on this property, the paper proves the existence of a Nash equilibrium. Moreover, the paper shows that, under competition, retailers tend to overstock relative to the centralized solution. Existence of an equilibrium is based on a result in Lippman and McCardle [67]. The latter studies a model of inventory competition between newsvendor retailers. Initial demand D is split among firms according to an exogenous splitting rule and excess demand is reallocated among the firms that have leftover inventory. For the case of two firms, $D = D_1 + D_2$, where D_i is the initial demand for firm i, $i = 1, 2$, and a fraction a_i of demand exceeding firm j's stocking level y_j is reallocated to firm i. Effective demand for firm i is $D_i + a_i(D_j - y_j)^+$. Firm i's profit function depends not only on its own stocking level, but also on the stock of the competing firm through the effective demand experienced by firm i. The paper shows that this two-firm newsvendor game is submodular and an equilibrium exists. It also extends the proof of existence of an equilibrium to the case of multiple firms.

Netessine and Rudi [84] and Boyaci [19] examine similar settings of competitive inventory management in which firms compete on product availability. That is, if a seller is out of stock, then a fraction of customer demand spills over a competing firm. The papers show that firms tend to overstock in this environment. In a multi-period setting, an out-of-stock situation may lead to either a lost sale, a backorder, or a customer switching to another seller. Netessine et al. [85] examine the impact of customers' response to stockouts on the equilibrium stocking quantities and profits. Li and Ha [65] and Caro and Martinez-de-Albeniz [27] study models of inventory-based competition in the context of accurate response and quick response strategies, respectively. Netessine and Zhang [86] consider a supply chain in which an upstream wholesaler sells to multiple competing newsvendor retailers. The upstream firm selects the wholesale price and the retailers choose their stocking quantities. In addition to vertical competition arising from the wholesaler's pricing decision, the paper considers two settings of horizontal competition — one in which retailers' products are substitutes and another in which they are complements. In the first setting, competition is modeled through stock-out based substitution. Instead, when products are complements, an increase in a retailer's stocking quantity stochastically increases demand for other retailers. The paper examines the horizontal externalities originated from retailer competition and concludes that in settings with complementary products, competition exacerbates the understocking that arises from double marginalization. In contrast, when products are substitutes, retailers tend to overstock, thereby compensating for the inefficiency brought by double marginalization. Cachon and Lariviere [22] study a setting in which retailer competition arises from the need to earn an adequate allocation of a supplier's limited capacity. The supplier operates under a turn-and-earn allocation scheme that bases a retailer's capacity allocation on past sales.

Another form of inventory competition arises when firms have the ability to transship excess inventory to satisfy demand in an out-of-stock location. In those settings, the firms' stocking decisions are interrelated. In the case of a stock-out, a firm may have access to additional inventory transshipped from another firm with excess inventory. Dong and Rudi [40] consider a manufacturer selling to multiple newsvendor retailers that are centrally managed. The manufacturer determines the wholesale price and the retailers jointly select their stocking quantities and can transship excess inventory. Competition with the manufacturer leads to the kind of vertical externalities discussed in Section 1.2. Rudi et al. [99] study a horizontally decentralized setting with two locations that can transship excess inventory at extra cost if the other location is out of stock.

The papers discussed in this section illustrate two of the most common sources of horizontal competition — through prices (without stock-out-based substitution) or through inventory availability (with fixed retail prices). The papers by Zhao and Atkins [115] and Xu and Hopp [113] explore newsvendor settings in which firms compete both through prices and inventory availability. Price competition arises naturally in the retail market as firms continuously gauge their competitors' prices to try to match them or to offer even more attractive prices. Inventory competition, on the other hand, presumes that firms can monitor their competitors' prevailing inventory levels. However, it turns out that, in many settings, the effect of inventory competition is relatively modest, especially when price is also a decision variable. Huh et al. [54] show that when the retailers' fill rates are in the 95%–99% range, stock-out based competition has a small effect on firms' decisions. That is, retailers can just stock their base-stock levels ignoring whatever their competitors do and still get close to what they would achieve by being strategic. This effect may be particularly noteworthy as in one can question the realism of information assumptions required by players to pursue equilibrium strategies.

1.4 Models with Risk Preferences

There are papers in the supply chain and related literature that look at risk averse players and the effect on order quantities and contract parameters. We provide a brief discussion here. Agrawal and Seshadri [2] study a supply chain with one supplier and multiple independent non-competing retailers where every agent maximizes the expectation of a concave utility function. They show that performance of the supply chain is improved if there exists a risk-neutral intermediate agent taking all the risks. Spulber [104] studies a similar model with a single supplier selling to multiple non-competing retailers. They show that in the setting with a risk-neutral agent, the risk-neutral agent takes all the risks to achieve supply-chain coordination. However, if no risk-neutral agent exists in the system, all agents share the risks. Gan et al. [46] study a supply chain with a single supplier and a single retailer, and model risk aversion by the expected exponential utility objective and the mean–variance objective. They show that the agents share risks under coordinating contracts in both cases. All these studies show that coordination is achieved when the agents share the risks unless a risk-neutral agent exists in the system. In contrast, Chen et al. [30] find that when the agents consider CVaR (Conditional Value at Risk), coordination can be achieved only when the least risk-averse agent takes all the risks. The general message is somewhat clear: When risk-averse agents exist in a supply chain, the nature of the contracts starts to matter a whole lot more than in systems with risk neutral players. The simple reason is that some contracts are more effective at allocating risks appropriately among the different players. The technique used to model risk aversion also matters, that is, CVaR produces different results than a general concave utility function. Choi et al. [35] consider risk aversion in a single-supplier, single-newsvendor-retailer setting, both under decentralized and centralized control. In the context of inventory competition, Shi et al. [101] examine the existence of Nash equilibria when the newsvendor retailers are risk averse.

1.5   Assembly Systems

Vertical and horizontal interactions are also prevalent in assembly systems. There is an abundant literature in operations management exploring pricing and capacity decisions in decentralized assembly systems. In these systems, the upstream tier consists of multiple independent firms, producing and delivering components that are subsequently assembled by a downstream firm. The assembler establishes a contract with the suppliers that indirectly determines the suppliers' capacity decisions. In turn, suppliers produce components, all of which are required to make the final product. Therefore, the total quantity assembled and sold to the market depends on the suppliers' collective production capacity decisions. In single-product assembly systems, complementarity of the suppliers' components facilitates the use of supermodular game techniques to compute and compare equilibria. Figure 1.3 below illustrates this setting.

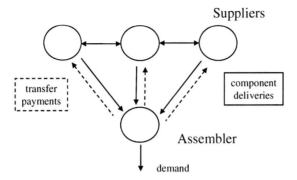

Fig. 1.3 Assembly system.

The assembly models described above typically assume that there is a single supplier for each component — i.e., no competition at the component level. Another stream of papers explores issues of supplier management in which multiple suppliers (or servers) of the same component compete for an allocation of the buyer's business. We provide a brief review of work on these issues. Ha et al. [52] study a buyer acquiring components from two suppliers in a deterministic setting. Suppliers compete either in terms of delivery frequency, with the buyer setting the prices, or in terms of the prices of their components, with the buyer setting the delivery frequency. The buyer allocates demand based on the suppliers' service delivery or price choices. Cachon and Zhang [25] study performance-based competition. Suppliers compete for the delivery of the same product or service, and the buyer allocates demand to suppliers according to their delivery speeds. In the remainder of this section, we focus on papers examining competition in multi-component assembly systems as depicted in Figure 1.3.

Wang and Gerchak [110] examine the impact of decentralization in an assembly system. All the suppliers and the assembler make capacity decisions. Due to the complementarity of their actions, the firm with the lowest capacity dictates the available capacity in the system. This is the essential property that drives the equilibrium results. While the firms' individual optimal capacities are nondecreasing in their component prices, in equilibrium, all firms choose the same capacity level equal to the lowest capacity in the system. The authors consider two contracting sequences that result in different equilibrium capacity decisions and profits. In the first setting, representative of industries with large manufacturers, the assembler acts as the Stackelberg leader, deciding the component prices to pay to the suppliers. In the second setting, the suppliers move first by setting their individual component prices. The effects of production and assembly costs and of the number of suppliers differ substantially in the two decentralized settings. This finding again illustrates how the order of play (arising possibly, in this case, as a result of the power structure in the supply chain) may impact the firms' equilibrium decisions and profits. The paper identifies a capacity-subsidy contract that can coordinate the assembly system under certain conditions. Tomlin [106] studies linear and piecewise linear price schedules in a similar assembly setting. Other papers exploring decentralized assembly systems include Gerchak and Wang [47], Gurnani and Gerchak [50] who consider the effect of random yield in the suppliers' production quantities, Fang et al. [44], and Bernstein and DeCroix [9], who explore issues of system design in a modular assembly setting. Bernstein et al. [11] study the impact of decentralized decision making on the behavior of multi-product assembly systems. Specifically, they consider a system where three components (two product-specific and one common) are used to produce two end-products to satisfy stochastic customer demands. The paper studies the system under both centralized and decentralized decision making, and focuses on the impact of decentralization on the use of commonality and hedging strategies.

In an infinite horizon setting, Bernstein and DeCroix [10] explore the impact of lead times and availability of inventory information on the performance of the firms in an assembly system. As in Cachon and Zipkin [26], the paper studies two games that differ in the way the firms track inventory. In the local game, all firms track their local (on-hand) inventory. In the echelon game, all firms are committed to tracking echelon inventory. The paper analyzes and compares the equilibria that arise in these games. It also describes a payment scheme between the assembler and the suppliers that allows the decentralized system to achieve the centralized solution. Bernstein and Kök [16] consider a decentralized assembly system in which a buyer purchases components from several first-tier suppliers over a finite horizon. Demand is deterministic. The paper examines the suppliers' investments in cost reduction initiatives under a contract that dynamically stipulates the components' purchase prices in every period. The paper models the suppliers' investment decisions under this contract as a dynamic game in closed-loop strategies. It is shown that there always exists an equilibrium in which the suppliers' investments are synchronized, that is, in each period either all suppliers invest in process improvement or no supplier does. Bernstein et al. [17] investigate the benefits of establishing a knowledge sharing network in a decentralized assembly system. Suppliers first non-cooperatively determine their investment in process improvement activities to reduce fixed operating costs. Subsequently, the assembler establishes a knowledge sharing network that facilitates the exchange of best practices among suppliers. This is modeled as a cooperative game in which, as a result of cooperation, all suppliers achieve reductions in their fixed costs from the knowledge sharing activities.

The above papers focus on the incentive distortion issues arising in assembly systems. It is not difficult to observe that the assembler in the role of a principal can dictate an appropriate contract that can end the distortion caused by competing suppliers. However, due to complementarity of the components and the unique role of the different players, the division of profits that a specific contract arrives at depends on the relative bargaining power of the players. Further, as is often seen in such systems, players can resort to strategies outside of the contract, such as strategic collusion, to increase their stake in the supply chain's profits. In Section 2 we explore this issue in greater detail.

1.6 Larger Networks

A number of papers have looked at vertical and horizontal interaction between firms in larger supply-chain networks. Corbett and Karmarkar [37] consider a multi-tier supply chain with multiple competing firms in each tier. Market demand is deterministic and linear in quantity, that is, the linear inverse demand function is $p = a - bQ$, where Q is the total quantity sold and a and b are constant parameters.

Firms in the same tier engage in quantity or Cournot competition. Each firm i selects a selling quantity q_i to maximize its profit, given that tier's resulting selling price $p = a - b(q_i + Q_{-i})$, where $Q_{-i} = \sum_{j \neq i} q_j$ is the aggregate quantity sold by firm i's competitors, and given the upstream input price. That is, firms in the same tier interact through their quantity decisions. The resulting aggregate equilibrium quantity is a function of the input price and affects the input price of the firms in the next downstream tier. Vertical interaction occurs as a result of the derived demand curve for the input. As demonstrated in Corbett and Karmarkar, the solution procedure entails solving for prices and quantities backwards from the most downstream to the most upstream tiers in the supply chain. For a given input price, firms in the same tier select their quantities according to a Nash equilibrium. The upstream input firms act as Stackelberg leaders, setting their price in anticipation of the aggregate equilibrium purchase of the downstream firms. Because downstream demand is linear, the derived equilibrium inverse demand function at each stage is also linear. The paper establishes the existence of a price/quantity equilibrium. Based on these results, the paper further explores the impact of fixed entry costs on the structure of the supply chain (equilibrium number of firms in each tier). Cho [32] builds on the model of Corbett and Karmarkar [37] to study the effects of a horizontal merger of two firms located in the same tier on the outputs and profits of the merging firms and of all other firms in the same or upstream/downstream tiers of the decentralized supply chain. A merging of two firms reduces the competitive intensity at the tier where the merging occurs and, at the same time, leads to a reduction of the marginal cost of the merged firm.

Also within the scope of vertical and horizontal competition, Carr and Karmarkar [28] examine a broader supply chain in which multiple sectors of firms within a tier produce different component that are subsequently assembled by other downstream firms. Each firm in a sector selects a production quantity to maximize its profit, given the input price, the quantities produced by other firms in the sector, and the decisions made by firms in other (complementary) sectors within the same tier. The paper develops an equilibrium concept defined as *coordinated successive Cournot* to derive the equilibrium prices and quantities of all firms. In a setting similar to those of Corbett and Karmarkar [37] and Carr and Karmarkar [28], and using a similar solution procedure, Majumder and Srinivasan [71] consider the effect of contract leadership on the efficiency of supply chains. The location of the Stackelberg leader within the supply network determines the contract sequence and, therefore, the resulting equilibrium prices and quantities. The paper finds that a leading firm earns a higher profit than its followers. The optimal location of the Stackelberg leader (in terms of supply-chain efficiency) depends on the demand and cost parameters. Adida and DeMiguel [1] study competition in a supply-chain setting with multiple manufacturers that supply products to a set of risk-averse retailers. In a model of Stackelberg competition, manufacturers determine the supply quantities in anticipation of the retailers' order quantities and the resulting market clearing wholesale prices. The paper analyzes the firms' equilibrium strategies and explores the extent of supply chain efficiency — i.e., the ratio of profit in the decentralized system to the optimal profit in the centralized system. There is, in fact, a stream of research quantifying the efficiency of decentralized supply chains — the so-called price of anarchy — in several models of vertical and horizontal competition (see Perakis and Roels [90] and the references therein).

1.7 Modeling Negotiation Power

Power in a supply-chain manifests itself in several ways. In many supply-chain models which use a Stackelberg game framework, the Stackelberg leader enjoys a certain amount of power simply by virtue of being the first mover who dictates the terms of the contract as, for example, in Majumder and Srinivasan. The advantage bestowed by being a leader is subtle and difficult to fully characterize. We illustrate this by using a few examples. Consider a simple supplier–retailer game where the retailer sets the final price p and faces a linear demand $a - bp$. Assume the supplier sells to the retailer at a wholesale price w per unit and we normalize the production cost to zero. In a pure Stackelberg game where the supplier acts as a leader and sets a wholesale price anticipating the retailer's reaction, it can be easily verified that, in equilibrium, the supplier earns two-thirds of the channel's profit and the retailer earns one-third. If we allow a larger contract space, say a wholesale price and a transfer payment T, then the supplier can simply extract as much of the channel's profit as possible, the retailer's reservation level being the only constraint. If the demand at the retailer has a different form, say, a simple downward sloping demand curve with constant price elasticity ap^{-b}, then using a wholesale price, the supplier gets 50% of the channel's profit. This simple example shows that the advantage of being a leader hinges on many factors such as the demand elasticity and the contracting space. (Related observations are found in Wang and Gerchak [110] and in Bernstein and Federgruen [13].)

Now consider a different example, where two suppliers sell (partially) differentiated products through a common retailer who sets retail prices for both products and faces market demand. Assume that a wholesale price contract is used. Here, a Stackelberg–Nash game is employed to study the interactions. Choi [34] shows a variety of surprising results. The ones relevant to this discussion are those that show that a Stackelberg leader in this setting may actually be worse off than the follower and this depends on the demand shape. In summary, although Stackelberg games may be a chosen mode of modeling channel interactions and power structures, one needs to be very careful on how this is done. Further, if one looks at interactions between a single supplier and single retailer, since there are no outside options endogeneous to the model, one can argue that a Stackelberg setting which endows the leader the power to set contract terms unilaterally may be somewhat inappropriate.

Within the framework of non-cooperative games in two-stage supply chains, an approach to modeling bargaining power is to assume that the retailers have an exogenous reservation profit level below which they will not participate in the supply chain. These reservation profit levels are usually assumed to represent the profit that the retailers could achieve by pursuing another opportunity outside the supply chain. Furthermore, they are often assumed to be exogenous, that is, independent of the negotiation process and of the retailers' opportunities within the supply chain. Ertogral and Wu [43] consider a setting with one supplier and one buyer, and model the process of contract negotiation with the presence of outside opportunities for both firms. Caruana and Einav [29] show that in a model with switching costs, players may have commitment power, that is, the ability to stake a position of power, even without having a first-mover advantage.

In a supply chain with one supplier selling to two competing retailers, Bernstein and Marx [18] investigate the effect of retailer bargaining power in the allocation of total supply-chain profit among all channel members, using a non-cooperative game approach. The paper models bargaining power by endowing retailers with the ability to set their reservation profit levels. A retailer's reservation profit level is the minimum amount of profit it requires to participate in the supply chain and carry the supplier's product. By making the reservation profit level an endogenous variable, this quantity not only reflects the retailer's opportunity outside the supply chain, but also its bargaining position within the supply chain relative to the competing retailer. The supplier and the retailers trade under a revenue sharing contract. A fully integrated firm (horizontally and vertically) would sell positive quantities at both retail outlets. When wholesale prices are w_1 and w_2 and both retailers are active (sell the supplier's product), let $\Pi(w_1, w_2)$ denote the joint payoff of all three firms. This joint payoff attains a maximum of $\Pi^* \equiv \Pi(w_1^*, w_2^*)$, where $w_i^* = \arg\max_{w_i \geq 0} \Pi(w_i, w_{3-i}^*)$. When only retailer i is active and the wholesale price is w_i, let $\Pi(w_i, \infty)$ be the overall joint payoff of the supplier and retailer i. The overall joint profit maximum in this case is $\Pi_i^m \equiv \Pi(w_i^m, \infty)$, where $w_i^m = \arg\max_{w_i \geq 0} \Pi(w_i, \infty)$. In contrast to the case in which both retailers are active, the joint-profit maximizing wholesale price with only one active retailer equals marginal cost.

Under revenue-sharing contracts, Cachon and Lariviere [23] show that any profit-sharing contract of the form $w_i^* = c_i - \xi_i^*$, with $\xi_i^* = \frac{\partial R_{3-i}}{\partial q_i}(q^*)$, and a revenue-sharing parameter $0 < \alpha \leq \frac{R_i(q^*) - c_i q_i^*}{R_i(q^*) - (c_i - \xi_i^*) q_i^*}$, coordinates the supply chain, where q^* is the integrated optimal stocking quantity vector. The vector (w_1^*, w_2^*) maximizes $\Pi(w_1, w_2)$ for any revenue-sharing parameters α_i, $i = 1, 2$. If each retailer's alternative to accepting the supplier's offer is to have profit given by an *exogenous* reservation profit level, then the supplier can extract all profit in the channel above the retailers' exogenous profits through the appropriate choice of the revenue-sharing parameters. With endogenous reservation profit levels, the retailers establish their reservation profit levels after learning the supplier's wholesale price offers. As in Muthoo [77], reputational concerns bind the retailers not to trade with the supplier if they cannot obtain a profit at least equal to their reservation profit. Thus, a retailer can credibly commit not to trade with the supplier if it does not receive a minimum level of profit from the transaction. In response to the reservation profit levels, the supplier sets the revenue-sharing parameters, essentially determining how system profits will be allocated. Finally, each retailer chooses the quantity to purchase from the supplier, which is zero if its reservation profit level constraint is not met. As one might expect, in this environment, the supplier's equilibrium profit is reduced relative to the setting with exogenous reservation profit levels and channel profit is not maximized. Allowing retailers to determine their reservation profit levels effectively increases their bargaining power, and so reduces the amount of surplus that the supplier is able to capture. When retailers determine their reservation profit levels, they can extract their incremental contribution to the channel. If only one retailer sells the supplier's product in equilibrium, then it is clear that channel profit is not maximized. If both retailers sell the supplier's product, then retailer 1's incremental contribution is $\Pi(w_1, w_2) - \Pi(\infty, w_2)$ and retailer 2's incremental contribution is $\Pi(w_1, w_2) - \Pi(w_1, \infty)$. If both retailers capture their incremental contributions, then the supplier's payoff is $\Pi(w_1, \infty) + \Pi(\infty, w_2) - \Pi(w_1, w_2)$, which has maximum at wholesale prices less than (w_1^*, w_2^*), and so channel profit is not maximized. The paper shows that the maximum supplier's profit is $\min\{\Pi_1^m, \Pi_2^m\}$. These observations indicate that a retailer's bargaining power may affect the portion of supply-chain profit that it claims for itself. Moreover, the results in Bernstein and Marx suggest that when retailers have bargaining power, a supplier's product may be sold through only one retailer, even when the maximization of channel profit requires that the supplier's product be sold through both retailers. Marx and Shaffer [72, 73] obtain similar results, but in their model reservation profit levels are exogenous and equal to zero and the retailers have all the bargaining power, including the ability to set the wholesale price.

Let us now consider a setting with two retailers that face random demand and purchase inventory from a common supplier. Competition between the retailers is modeled as in the competing newsvendor model of Lipman and McCardle [67]. Assume initial firm demands D_1 and D_2 are independent, and each is uniformly distributed on $[0,1]$. Denote aggregate demand by $D \equiv D_1 + D_2$. Since the retailers' products are substitutes, a proportion of the unsatisfied demand at each retailer may try to purchase the product from the other retailer. Thus, effective demand for retailer i is given by $D_i^e = D_i + s[D_j - y_j]^+$, where y_j denotes the inventory level of retailer j, and s, $0 < s \leq 1$, is the proportion of excess demand at one retailer that substitutes at the other retailer. That is, s measures the degree of substitutability between the retailers' products. (Lipman and McCardle [67], introduce this example for the case $s = 1$.) Assume that the unit selling price is $p = 2$ and the unit production cost is $c = 1$. The wholesale price charged to retailer i is given by $w_i \in [1,2]$. When only one retailer is active, it serves the entire market and $\Pi(w_i, \infty)$ is maximized when $w_i = 1$, with $\Pi_i^m = 1/2$. If both retailers are active, the equilibrium inventory levels increase with the substitution coefficient s. Applying the results in Bernstein and Marx, it is shown that both retailers are active in equilibrium, but the revenue sharing contract that arises in equilibrium does not coordinate the system. Furthermore, the supplier's equilibrium profit is always below $\Pi_1^m = \Pi_2^m = 1/2$. As the retailers become stronger substitutes (higher s), their equilibrium reservation profit levels increase, while the supplier's equilibrium profit decreases. At the same time, system efficiency (system profit under the equilibrium contract versus centralized profit) decreases with s. Stronger competition between the retailers increases their bargaining power by increasing aggregate downstream inventory.

To conclude, we discussed how Stackelberg leadership endows players with intrinsic power. In certain settings, manipulating reservation levels can also be a tool in modeling power. The preceding discussion gives way to the next question we address in this review. Namely, the role of the bargaining process and the firms' negotiation power on the terms of the contract that is eventually adopted in the supply chain which, in turn, affects the division of supply-chain profit. There are a number of ways one might try to formalize the bargaining process and the firms' negotiation power in a supply chain. We provide a discussion on these issues in the next section.

2

Negotiation Power and Cooperative Bargaining

2.1 Introduction

The previous section discussed several incentive issues that arise in supply chains and used a non-cooperative game theoretic framework to analyze some of the interaction between players in such settings. In the current section, we will take a related but different approach. We will look at how one can adopt a cooperative bargaining approach to resolve some of these issues. We will also relate, whenever appropriate, the results from taking such an approach to the theory of industrial organization. Before we dive into the bargaining approach, it may help clarify the contents of the upcoming section and its place in the literature in operations that apply cooperative games. The latter is a fairly large and growing literature. Broadly speaking, its aim is somewhat related to what we explore in this section, that is, how do players allocate costs and profits within a supply chain. As one can imagine, there are at least two ways in which one can approach the problem of allocations, first being the prescriptive route which suggests useful allocations to players so they can jointly achieve a common good and the allocation is such that no one has an incentive to defect. This is exactly the idea of the Core [48], a concept widely applied in the operations literature. The Core tackles the following issue. Consider N players engaged in joint actions that create a certain surplus (payoff). Core is a solution concept that looks at how this surplus should be divided between the players so that the grand coalition, which achieves the highest surplus, is sustained. In other words, the core is the set of allocations under which no coalition has a value greater than the sum of its members' payoffs. Therefore, no coalition has incentive to leave the grand coalition and receive a larger payoff. Calculating core allocations and advising players to use them is a prescriptive approach. Early papers on this topic are Wang and Parlar [109], Hartman et al. [53], and Meca et al. [75]. The latter also gives a good survey of the literature. (We refer to Cachon and Netessine [24] for an extensive review of game theoretical models in supply-chain analysis, including cooperative game theory.) Our approach here is slightly different. We assume that players negotiate over allocations (or terms of trade). We consider a well-studied model that predicts the outcome of negotiations and use that to describe how allocations in supply-chains may be arrived at, if players negotiate. Therefore, this section is by no means a review of cooperative game theory and its applications in operations. It is specifically targeted at models that use bargaining as the main tool.

Our motivation for using a bargaining approach is manifold. First of all, it is not hard to imagine that terms of trade between supply-chain partners are often negotiated rather than simply arrived at using a non-cooperative take-it-or-leave-it type of approach. Therefore, modeling contract negotiations seems quite natural. Second, as we will argue later in this section, in most settings studied in the operations literature where players are risk neutral and are endowed with full information, the system-wide efficient outcome will usually prevail. The important issue is how this surplus is divided as a result of some bargaining process between players. Adopting a bargaining paradigm allows us to understand finer details of this issue. Third, from a higher level theoretical perspective, there is a broad division of game theory into two approaches: the cooperative and the non-cooperative approach. These approaches, though different in their theoretical content and the methodology used in their analysis, are really just two different ways of looking at the same problem. To quote the words of Aumann: "the game is one ideal and the cooperative and non-cooperative approaches are two shadows." The *program of Nash*, which we describe later attests to the same fact. Therefore, it is of theoretical interest to researchers to relate findings from adopting a cooperative bargaining approach to those obtained by using the traditional approach seen in supply-chain research.

The rest of this section is organized as follows. We first review some fundamentals of cooperative bargaining. We pay particular attention to how this model can be used as a prototype to analyze some of the models discussed in Section 1. Following this discussion, we analyze the atomic model, that is, a single supplier selling to a single newsvendor-type retailer. We then move to more complicated multi-tier systems and describe some new bargaining solution concepts that have been recently developed to deal with such models. We conclude by describing future research directions and discuss some relevant problems for which we do not currently have solution procedures.

2.2 A Bargaining Model: Nash Bargaining

In the following discussion of bargaining, we will mainly use a cooperative framework and employ the model of Nash [80]. Although the concept of cooperation is important and somewhat easy to fathom, it is somewhat subtle when one wants to model cooperative behavior. The dictionary definition of cooperation is "to act together with a common purpose." However, this definition does not describe the incentive issues that arise when players try to cooperate. Would, for instance, individuals have to set aside their separate utility functions and create a new one that describes their collective utility? We know from the literature on social choice that such a conceptual framework is both difficult to construct and often infeasible to work with. With this in mind, Nash [81] proposed that cooperation between players can be studied using the same basic concepts of non-cooperative equilibrium. Nash argues that cooperative actions between players are a result of some process of bargaining among "cooperating" players and in any such process, every player will behave as a self-interested utility-maximizing agent as in any non-cooperative game. This results in the *Nash program* for cooperative games. The Nash program, simply put, is a principle that calls for suitable modification of the underlying game so that its Nash equilibrium when viewed as a strategic game is the same as the cooperative solution when viewed as a cooperative game. Next, we describe the Nash bargaining solution concept.

For simplicity, let us assume we have two players. Nash starts by considering a set A of possible agreements. This set can take many forms. It could simply be quantities, prices, allocations of profits or more complicated contractual forms. It is important to note that these are merely objects over which players negotiate and that each player has a preference ordering on this set. In case of breakdown in negotiations, an event D occurs. The risk propensity of the two players is quite important in this game. Each player's preference therefore has to be defined not just on the set of agreements, but on all possible lotteries of those agreements (i.e., on the convex hull of the set A). Although there is little to no explicit risk in the way this has been described so far, the underlying uncertainty and the risk of breakdown in any negotiation process motivates the players' attitude. Each player's preference is assumed to satisfy the standard assumptions demanded by von Neumann and Morgenstern [108] and consequently each player has an underlying utility $u_i : A \cup D \to \Re$. Next, we define F to be the set of utility allocations of the possible agreements, i.e., $F = \{(u_1(a), u_2(a)) : a \in A\}$, and d the disagreement payoff allocation or the disagreement point, i.e., $d = (u_1(D), u_2(D))$. Formally, Nash defined a two-person bargaining problem (which can be extended easily to more than two players) as consisting of a pair $\langle F, d \rangle$, where F is a subset of $\Re^2$ and $d = (d_1, d_2)$ is a vector in $\Re^2$. F is convex, closed, nonempty, and bounded. The disagreement point may capture the utility of the opportunity profit. Nash looked for a bargaining solution — i.e., an outcome in the feasible set that satisfied a set of axioms. The axioms ensure that the solution is symmetric (identical players receive identical utility allocations), feasible (the sum of the allocations does not exceed the total pie), Pareto optimal (it is impossible for both players to improve their utilities over the bargaining solutions), and the solution needs to be preserved under linear transformations and be independent of "irrelevant" alternatives. We refer the reader to Roth [95] for a very good description of the solution approach and a more detailed explanation of the axioms. The remarkable result due to Nash is that there is a bargaining solution that satisfies the above axioms and it is unique!

Theorem 2.1. [81] There is a unique solution that satisfies all the "axioms." This solution, for every two person bargaining game $\langle F, d \rangle$, is obtained by solving

$$\arg \max_{x=(x_1,x_2)\in F, x\geq d} (x_1 - d_1)(x_2 - d_2).$$

The axiomatic approach, though simple, can be used as a building block for much more complex bargaining problems. Even though the axiomatic approach is prescriptive, descriptive non-cooperative models of negotiation such as the Nash demand game [96] and the alternating offer game [98] reach similar conclusions as Nash bargaining. This fits in with the Nash program and demonstrates the robustness of the Nash bargaining solution. Within the scheme of cooperative games, there are several other bargaining models. Some of these are modifications to Nash's model by adding or relaxing some of the axioms. Others prescribe a ordinal versus a cardinal utility model between preferences. An excellent review of the various models is available in Roth [95]. We do not review these models in this manuscript for two reasons. First, much of the spirit of the discussion that follows does not change with many of the cooperative models of negotiation. Second, almost all the papers in the literature in operations use the model by Nash. Finally, it is noteworthy to mention that there is some empirical evidence to the validity of Nash bargaining solutions in predicting outcomes of buyer–seller negotiations. Neslin and Greenhalgh [82, 83] study the Nash bargaining solution in the purchase of advertising media time. They find that negotiated buyer–seller settlements are close to the predictions of Nash. Eliashberg [41] show the robustness of the Nash bargaining solution in accurately predicting outcomes of a marketing channel laboratory simulation, where price and quantity are negotiated.

2.3   Applying the Nash Bargaining Model

A major objective of this section will be to explore bargaining models in supply-chain settings. To do this, we first explore how the Nash model can be applied to some simple settings and what are some underlying issues of interest from a modeling perspective. We start with perhaps the simplest model used in the operations literature, the atomic model, with a single supplier selling to a newsvendor-type buyer who faces uncertain demand. To make the situation concrete, let us assume the basic model used in Lariviere and Porteus [64], but now the supplier and buyer negotiate the terms of trade. Using the same contractual terms from the above paper, the set A of possible agreements will now include all feasible values of w, the wholesale price, and Q, the quantity transferred between the two players. Let us assume that both players are risk neutral. Therefore the set F is the expected profit for each player for every possible value of w and Q and all possible lotteries. It is immediate that F is a convex set. We let d be zero, that is, the utility to each player of the disagreement outcome is zero. It is fairly straightforward to notice several properties of the Nash bargaining outcome. First of all, the players will reach the efficient outcome simply by virtue of the Pareto optimality requirement. This also makes good practical sense, there is no reason for rational players to leave money on the table when negotiating terms of trade. Therefore, channel coordination is somewhat moot. If we do not make any further specifications, we also know that the above optimization problem over F will yield equal allocations to the players. Therefore the supplier and buyer will each earn half the first-best profit. Note that we started by negotiating over objects in A. Thus, the negotiated contract outcome will be the unique (w, Q) that gets each player the above allocations. In this simple example, the contractual outcome is unique, but this is not always the case as the mapping from the set A to F need not be one-to-one in general.

An immediate observation from the above description is that the wholesale price here simply works as a lump sum transfer. One could have simply constructed a game where the terms of trade include the quantity exchanged and a transfer payment and arrived at a similar outcome. This echoes the discussion in the earlier section of how the above system can be coordinated with a wholesale price set equal to marginal cost and a side payment. To continue the discussion along these lines from the earlier section, we have not yet addressed how the bargaining solution reflects the relative bargaining powers of the two players. We attend to this in the following section.

2.4 Bargaining Power

Indeed, an equal split of the profit only makes sense when neither player has outside opportunities and both are equally powerful. Within the context of the Nash bargaining framework, we have few things to manipulate in the primitives that can model power. We have exactly two objects. First, the axioms themselves. Second, the underlying utility of the players or the value of the disagreement point. Since the latter will mean we may have to forego risk neutrality, for now, we will think of the first option. Dropping the symmetry requirement in the axioms yields a family of bargaining solutions

$$\arg \max_{x \in F, x \geq d} (x_1 - d_1)^\alpha (x_2 - d_2)^\beta$$

with $\alpha + \beta = 1$. The negotiated solutions are now parameterized by α which can be thought of as the relative negotiation power of a player, $\alpha = 1$ being an omnipotent player. For instance, when two players with zero disagreement values negotiate on allocations of \$1, the above solution implies that the first player gets $x_1 = \alpha$ and the second player receives $x_2 = 1 - \alpha = \beta$. This class of solutions is known as the *generalized Nash bargaining* (GNB) solutions. Another simple route is manipulating the value of the disagreement outcome, with the interpretation that it is an outside option that players have. Similar to the discussion in Section 1.7, but somewhat more direct, the value of disagreement points, when interpreted as reservation profits and not as actual costs, directly endows players with a higher negotiating power. It must be clear to the reader that in a simple two person bargaining game, the allocation to a player of the total pie linearly increases with the value of the disagreement outcome of that player.

A related and interesting interpretation of power within the Nash bargaining context was developed by Muthoo [77], who provides a natural interpretation of the indices α and β in the GNB. Muthoo uses what are referred to as commitment tactics. The main idea in such models is that before embarking on some negotiation process (Nash bargaining, in our case), players take actions that partially commit them to certain bargaining positions. The meaning of the commitment is that a player is unwilling to accept a share smaller than the announced commitment. Commitment tactics preserve the simple structure of the Nash bargaining solution. It is important to note that the commitment is not directly related to the disagreement point. However, it is evident that each of the players will commit to a share that is not smaller than their disagreement points. Actually, it seems natural to expect the players to inflate their commitments and thus increase their share of the pie. But, in doing so the players need to exercise some caution because if the sum of the commitments is larger than the pie, and if the bargaining process is to have a non-trivial solution, at least one of the players must revoke his commitment. Revoking such a partial commitment is costly. It could, for instance, be attributed to or construed as a loss of credibility. After such partial commitments have been made, the players engage in the Nash bargaining process to strike a deal and arrive at their allocations. Simultaneously, they try to minimize the extent to which they must revoke their commitments. Muthoo's model ties in this cost of revoking a commitment to the index α of the generalized bargaining model. Such commitment tactics are not unusual and often signal a player's bargaining power. Bacharach and Lawler [7], Schelling [100], and Cutcher-Gershenfeld et al. [39] discuss the role of these tactics and give examples from industry. For a paper that uses this idea in contract negotiations, we refer to Nagarajan and Bassok [78].

In the preceding discussion, we discussed how power can be modeled and interpreted in the context of Nash bargaining using the indices in the objective function of the GNB game. As mentioned, to model power in the context of Nash bargaining, we can look at one of two things, the axioms that dictate the bargaining solution or the inputs (players' preferences, disagreement outcomes, etc.) The GNB discussed above takes the first approach and relaxes the symmetry axiom. We have also discussed models that use the approach of using the reservation profit levels (the disagreement outcomes in Nash bargaining) in different settings. The advantage of these two approaches that do not tinker with the utility of the players is that we preserve risk neutrality. As the readers may appreciate, this allows researchers to avoid quite a bit of analytical tedium. We now discuss the second approach, that is, changing the utility of players to model power. We will later discuss models that explicitly analyze such settings. Before we go further, we note that as one may suspect in such cases, risk aversion endows a disadvantage to a player's bargaining position. More precisely, using measures of comparative risk aversion as suggested by Arrow [6], Pratt [94], and Yaari [114], it can be shown [97] that in a two-person bargaining problem, the Nash bargaining solution assigns a player increasing utilities as his opponent becomes more risk averse. Thus, a player's bargaining power increases as his opponent becomes more risk averse. This comparison strictly applies to two players, one which has a utility function that is a concave function of the other's utility function. Therefore, the above statements do not apply directly to two players with arbitrary risk aversion. This is somewhat of a disadvantage, but this is a restriction of the Nash bargaining concept.

With this background, we now discuss some papers that have exploited the above paradigm to analyze terms of trade in supply chains. Perhaps the earliest known instance of an application of cooperative bargaining in a supply chain context is the work by Kohli and Park [57]. The authors study a model in which a buyer and seller negotiate the terms of a quantity discount contract in an EOQ setting. The underlying negotiation model uses Nash bargaining and its variants proposed by Kalai and Smordinsky [55] and Eliashberg [41]. Moreover, the authors look at the issue of risk aversion among players and show in the context of their model how risk aversion leads to higher cost allocations. The authors study the allocations as a function of risk aversion as well as other sources of bargaining power discussed above. Gurnani and Shi [51] use a Nash Bargaining model to study a business-to-business supply chain. In particular, they study a setting in which a buyer and supplier negotiate over the price of a contract. The negotiated price, which is arrived at by a straightforward application of Nash Bargaining is then used to calculate the transaction quantity. Baron et al. [8] study a model where some of the terms of trade are negotiated in a supply chain. More precisely, they use the well-known model of McGuire and

Staelin [74] and explore what happens when parties negotiate over the wholesale price. Chod and Rudi [33] use Nash bargaining in a stage of a biform game that analyzes strategic investments in capacity. The above papers explore two of the possible routes we have discussed above to model power. Two papers that explore intrinsic channel power on re-negotiations are Plambeck and Taylor [92, 93]. They use negotiation to derive terms of trade ex-post to realization of uncertainty. Although an interesting application of negotiation, their papers are not directly related to the discussion in this section. A paper that explores how negotiated allocations, depending on the power of players, affect decisions on outsourcing and therefore the structure of the supply chain is Feng and Lu [45]. They use the GNB model to model power and derive the allocations accordingly.

2.5   Effects of Risk Aversion

In the previous section, we had looked at papers that discuss supply chains with risk averse players and the role of an intermediary and insurance. The analysis there was done using a non-cooperative framework. Let us now turn our attention to contract negotiation in the basic model we used earlier. We make a notable change — we let one of the players, say, the buyer, be risk averse and the seller continues to be risk neutral. Recall that when both players are risk neutral, it does not make sense to describe a game with a complicated set of terms of trade — rather, a simple allocation of shares will suffice. As one may suspect, this is no longer true when players are risk averse. To illustrate, let us assume that players negotiate the following terms of trade: w and Q, as before, and a buy-back parameter b. Effectively, the seller agrees to buy back unsold units from the buyer at a constant rate of b per unit. The feasible set and the disagreement points are as discussed in the previous section. As mentioned, the agents negotiate on a feasible set that represents expected utilities as a function of the vector $P = (w, b, Q)$. Let the buyer's utility be $u_b(\cdot)$, a strictly concave function. To introduce further notation, let the buyer's revenue per unit be s on products he sells, h be the per unit holding cost on unsold goods at the buyer, and let c be the per unit production cost to the seller. We then have that $P^* = (w^*, b^*, Q^*)$ yields the Nash bargaining solution. Moreover, $b^* = s + h$ and $F(Q^*) = (s - c)/(s + h)$, where w^* solves

$$\max_w \left\{ (w - c)Q^* - (s + h) \int_0^{Q^*} (Q^* - \varepsilon) f(\varepsilon) d\varepsilon \right\} \{u_R ([s - w]Q^*)\}.$$

First of all, notice that the buy-back rate moves the risk from the buyer to the seller. This aids in the choice of the buyer and seller agreeing to transact the quantity Q that corresponds to the first-best solution when both players are risk neutral. One can think of this as an insurance the risk neutral seller offers the buyer. In return, the wholesale price the players negotiate is the premium the buyer pays the seller. The wholesale price above can be shown to yield the seller a greater utility than when both players are risk neutral (i.e., the seller's net utility here is greater than 50% of the first-best profit when players are risk neutral). The seller is able to exploit the risk aversion of the buyer to improve his bargaining position. This directly ties to the fact that, in Nash bargaining, risk aversion is a disadvantage. As the risk aversion of the buyer increases, the seller's utility increases as well. The above is an example where we have essentially used a primitive of the bargaining game to model power.

The second insight one can get is by casting the above game with a variation on the terms of trade being negotiated. For instance, if one were to choose a revenue-sharing parameter instead of the buy-back price, then one could show that the results are different. In fact, the buy-back contract Pareto dominates the revenue-sharing contract: The bargaining solution under a buy-back contract allocates higher expected utilities to both players than under a revenue-sharing contract. When players are risk neutral, we know that these two contracts are identical, both in a cooperative bargaining game as well as in the non-cooperative version. These results, in spirit, can be replicated when both the buyer and seller are risk-averse and when the buyer's utility function is a concave function of the seller (although the order quantity is no longer the same). That is, the buy-back contract Pareto dominates the revenue-sharing contract and the seller offers insurance to the buyer through the buy-back parameter.

2.6 Bargaining Models for Multi-Player Systems

Thus far we have looked at negotiation games between two players organized in two tiers. We will discuss settings where there are multiple players in the tiers and with multiple tiers. The Nash bargaining solution as we have described it is for two players. However, as we have mentioned, the concept can be extended to N players with one caveat. Nash bargaining only models situations where players simultaneously agree to what are the possible objects being negotiated and the utility associated with each outcome (i.e., the sets A and F). Therefore, when N players across different tiers negotiate, the only setting where Nash bargaining can be directly applied is one where all players sit together, in a manner of speaking, and agree on one pie of utility outcomes. From a modeling perspective, for various reasons, this may not be very desirable. Negotiations may be done by different subsets of players and the outcomes of these may affect other negotiations. Moreover, in settings with multiple players in a network, information may be local. That is, players 1 and 2 and players 1 and 3 may agree on a mutually feasible pie but players 2 and 3 may not have anything to negotiate on directly. Further to this, there are often legal constraints. Consider a supplier selling goods to two competing retailers. These three players may not be allowed by law to hold joint negotiations and decide outcomes cooperatively. For settings such as these, we do not have an axiomatic bargaining paradigm that we can readily apply. In what follows, we will look at situations that call for extending the bargaining paradigm described above.

2.7 Two-Echelon Systems

We first look at two-tier supply chains with a single player in tier 1 selling to multiple buyers in tier 2. Consider a supply chain in which there is a single supplier selling to n retailers. Further, assume that these retailers do not compete in the same market. As before, we assume that the supplier and each individual retailer negotiate on a (w, b) contract in which the supplier sells to the retailer a certain quantity at the negotiated wholesale price, w, and accepts returns of unsold inventory at the buy-back price, b. We will assume for now that all retailers are risk neutral, but the use of a buy-back in our contracting space allows us to extend some of the results to risk-averse retailers as well. If the retailers are identical in all respects, the negotiation process becomes easy as the supply chain can be thought of as n copies of a supply chain with a single supplier and a single retailer, which we have dealt with earlier. If we suppose that the retailers are not identical (we will be more precise very soon), the negotiation process becomes less transparent. For one, the Robinson–Patman act requires that every retailer be given the same price contract. The bargaining process becomes more interesting due to this constraint. By way of illustrating this difficulty and to motivate our first game, consider a supply chain with a single supplier supplying to two non-competing retailers differentiated by their market selling prices. Assume that all parties are risk neutral and thereby maximize their expected profits. The supplier and retailers negotiate on the prices and each retailer orders a quantity that maximizes his expected profit at the negotiated price. Note that, in the absence of a legal constraint, each supplier–retailer channel will independently pick a price that coordinates the channel and splits the channel coordinated profit equally between the supplier and the respective retailer. We infer this from the results on Nash bargaining we discussed earlier. The outcome is not clear in the presence of a constraint, especially when the two retailers face different market selling prices. Indeed, it is not even clear if the two channels will pick prices that will coordinate them. In fact, there is no single clear negotiation process that is immediate to such a channel, but there are several possibilities. In the following discussion we propose one such game and deduce results for the single-supplier, multiple-retailer channel.

Let $I = \{1, 2, \ldots, n\}$ denote the set of retailers. In this game, we adopt a sequential bargaining model in which at each stage the negotiation between the participants is modeled as a Nash bargaining game. In the first stage, the supplier negotiates with the "first" retailer and arrives at a "price." We are rather loose with our nomenclature at this point. Let "price" represent a vector of negotiating instruments. For instance, the wholesale price, the buy-back price, and the quantity that the retailer buys from the supplier are possible parameters that could be negotiated by the parties. The parameters that the parties choose to negotiate are specified in each game. In any case, for simplicity, we bundle these parameters and call them "price." In the second stage of the game, the supplier does the same process with the "second" retailer and arrives at some new prices. In the nth stage of the game, the supplier negotiates with the last retailer and arrives at the nth set of prices. We do not allow for re-negotiation, but however require that each of the first $n-1$ retailers is no worse off when offered the nth prices compared to the prices they arrived at by negotiation in their respective stages. We further require that the resulting prices are such that the supplier is not interested in playing with any non-trivial subset of retailers. Indeed, the profit obtained by the supplier might depend on the sequence of the retailers in the negotiation process. If $\Pi(n)$ is the set of all permutations of the n retailers, the supplier will choose the "best" sequence. Let $\Theta(k)$ be the set of all subsets of I such that each subset has exactly k retailers. For $\lambda_i^k \in \Theta(k), i = 1, 2, \ldots, \binom{n}{k}$, let $\Pi(\lambda_i^k)$ be the set of all permutations of λ_i^k. Note that if, for some reason, the supplier plays with the set of retailers λ_i^k, then he will choose the best sequence from $\Pi(\lambda_i^k)$, which we denote as $\lambda^*(i, k)$. We denote the resulting prices as $P(\lambda^*(i, k))$. In a game in which the wholesale and buy-back prices are negotiated, we would have $P(\lambda^*(i, k)) = (w(\lambda^*(i, k)), b(\lambda^*(i, k)))$. In the game with the n retailers, let P_i denotes the prices at the end of the ith stage — i.e., when the supplier finishes negotiations with the ith retailer. Hence, P_n is the final price at the end of the negotiations and all the n retailers will accept this price. Finally, we denote $\pi_M^k(P_i)$ and $\pi_j(P_i)$ as the profit made by the supplier with the kth retailer, when the supplier offers the prices P_i to this retailer, and the profit made by the jth retailer at the same prices, respectively. We propose that the resulting prices P_n satisfy the following constraints:

$$\sum_{i=1}^{n} \pi_M^i(P_n) \geq \sum_{j \in \lambda_i^k} \pi_M^j(P(\lambda^*(i, k))), \quad \lambda_i^k \in \Theta(k), k = 1, 2, \ldots, n-1 \tag{2.1a}$$

$$\pi_j(P_n) \geq \pi_j(P_j) \qquad j = 1, 2, \ldots, n-1 \tag{2.1b}$$

$$\pi_j(P_j) \geq 0 \qquad j = 1, 2, \ldots, n-1 \tag{2.1c}$$

$$\pi_n(P_n) \geq 0.$$

The constraint (2.1a) ensures that the supplier will find it more profitable to trade with all the retailers and will not prefer to ignore any subset of retailers. Constraint (2.1b) ensures that with the final negotiated prices every retailer makes at least what he was "promised" at the end of his negotiations with the supplier. Note that we do not allow for re-negotiation and hence when the supplier returns to a retailer with whom he had negotiated earlier and forces the new and final price on him, the retailer will not have cause to complain. Constraint (2.1c) ensures that at no stage, retailers accept a negative allocation. The last constraint ensures that the last retailer, who will be visited exactly once, will participate. Note that, in this game, we have ignored explicit disagreement points that players may exogenously possess. We assume that these are zero. Rather, we have implicit disagreement points. That is, in the sequential game, a retailer in any stage of negotiation, will accept no less than what he was promised before. Thus, the disagreement points arise naturally at each step of the negotiation with the retailers.

The complete n-retailer game is described as follows. First of all, we look at the set of prices that satisfy the above four constraints. If this set is non-empty, then it is clear that it is in the interest of the supplier to trade with all the n retailers. Moreover, if the set is convex, we can find the resulting prices from the Nash bargaining game the supplier plays with the last retailer. If the set is not convex, we can do the same using the largest convex subset. However, if the set is empty, the supplier and the retailers cannot agree upon any payoffs (i.e., the feasible set is trivial) and hence all parties will get zero. At this stage, we cast aside the requirement to play with all the retailers and will formulate the same game with $n - 1$ retailers (as of yet we have not mentioned how we determine the retailer to be removed) and continue. This will continue until the feasible set becomes non-empty.

To illustrate this game and to get some insights on the "best" sequence for the supplier, we first consider the case of a single supplier and two retailers. Let the retailers be L, H, with L and H denoting lower and higher market selling prices, respectively, i.e., $s_L < s_H$. To describe the game, the supplier negotiates with the "first" retailer (which can be either L or H) and arrives at P_1. She then negotiates with the second (or the last) retailer in this case and they arrive at P_2, which is the common price that both retailers have to accept. To formulate the constraints of this game, we use the same notation as above, and let $\hat{\pi}_M^i$ denote the maximum profit the supplier would have obtained by trading with just one retailer:

$$\pi_M^1(P_2) + \pi_M^2(P_2) \geq \hat{\pi}_M^H/2 \tag{2.2a}$$

$$\pi_1(P_2) \geq \pi_1(P_1)(= \hat{\pi}_M^1/2) \tag{2.2b}$$

$$\pi_2(P_2) \geq 0. \tag{2.2c}$$

Note that (2.2b) is similar to (2.1a). The supplier is better with two active retailers than by just going with a single retailer. Assume that, in the aforementioned game, the parties negotiate on the wholesale price, the buy-back price, and the quantity that the individual retailers purchase from the supplier. More precisely, we let $P_i = (w_i, b_i, Q_i)$. The solution must satisfy the three constraints in (2.2). Further, let $\hat{Q}_i, i \in \{1, 2, H, L\}$ represent the channel coordinating quantity in the first and second channel (as per the sequence), or the quantity that coordinates the channel when the supplier trades only with H or L retailer as the case may be. Let $\pi^i(Q)$ be the total profit of the ith channel when the retailer orders Q from the supplier.

The description of this game is as follows: In the first stage, the supplier negotiates with the first retailer and they arrive at a price vector $P_1 = (w_1, b_1, Q_1)$. The supplier then negotiates with the second retailer and they subsequently arrive at $P_2 = (w_2, b_2, Q_2)$. The wholesale price and buy-back price from the second negotiation is carried back to the first retailer. We assume at this point that the first retailer still has to buy the quantity Q_1, though at the new prices (w_2, b_2). This assumption on the commitment of the order quantity is superfluous because, if at the end of the game the resulting prices are (w, b) and the quantities sold to the retailers are Q_1 and Q_2, respectively, then it can be shown that $Q_i = \hat{Q}_i$, $i = 1, 2$. Based on this, Nagarajan and Sosic [79] show that if (w, b) are the final prices and $\hat{Q}_i$ are the quantities sold to the retailers in the respective channels, then $\pi_M^i(w, b, \hat{Q}_i) = \pi_{R_i}(w, b, \hat{Q}_i) = \pi^i(\hat{Q}_i)/2$, for $i = 1, 2$. When there are more than two retailers, the constraint (2.1a) becomes binding — i.e., the manufacturer will usually choose to ignore some retailers.

We also find that the bargaining solution no longer coordinates every channel. However, using a different contract mechanism, such as an additional slotting fee (which allows for more flexibility), the results for the two retailer game can be mimicked in a n retailer setting. In the above example, we appealed to Nash bargaining for each of the two player bargaining games. We used a sequential framework and used constraints tied to disagreement outcomes to come up with a negotiated solution. Obviously, one could have proposed other solutions that may depend on the sequence of how negotiations are done or on other stipulations. In effect, we have to adopt such specifications as we do not have a ready-made solution procedure to use the Nash bargaining framework directly, other than to force all players to sit together and negotiate with some outside conditions imposed on the feasible set.

Continuing our discussion on multi-player systems, we next look at an assembly system, where the interaction between players gets stronger in the sense that all players are required for a useful outcome to emerge.

2.8   Assembly Systems

Let us consider an assembly system, in which N component suppliers sell individual components to a downstream assembler. As we have noted in the previous section, there is a significant literature on decentralized assembly systems. We will restrict ourselves here to the analysis in Nagarajan and Bassok [78], who use a sequential framework to study such systems. Nagarajan and Bassok [78] look at a supply chain with a single assembler who buys complementary components from n suppliers, assembles the final product, and sells it to his customers. Players take actions in the following sequence. First, (Stage 3) the suppliers form coalitions between themselves. Second, (Stage 2) the coalitions compete for a position in the bargaining sequence. Finally, (Stage 1) the coalitions negotiate with the assembler on the wholesale price and quantity of goods to be sold to the assembler. We will not discuss the coalition formation process or stability here, but rather focus on the bargaining issues. The paper assumes that the negotiation process is sequential, that is the assembler negotiates with one coalition at a time and the assembler has the power to determine the negotiation sequence, while the suppliers can freely form alliances. A criticism of using Nash bargaining to analyze such a system is the fact that there is dependence on the sequence of negotiation. Here is what we mean. Let α be the negotiation power of the assembler (the index in the generalized Nash bargaining game) and β be the power of any supplier (assume for illustration that all suppliers are equally powerful). To describe the feasible set in this game, we first introduce some notation. The negotiations between the suppliers and the assembler determine a share of Π^C, the efficient profit for each player. Also, throughout this discussion, we use x (with suitable subscripts) to denote variables in the bargaining game and (with suitable subscripts) to denote the solution of the bargaining process. Consider now the negotiations between the ith supplier and the assembler, i.e., the ith sub-stage. Let $x_{A,i}$ be the pie that the assembler and suppliers $i, i + 1, \ldots, n$ divide among themselves. Thus $x_{A,1}$, the pie to be allocated between the assembler and suppliers $1, \ldots, n$ is nothing but Π^C. Let x_i denote the share of the channel profit that the ith supplier receives. Since the generalized Nash bargaining solution is Pareto optimal, $x_{A,i+1} + x_i = x_{A,i}$. The feasible set for each sub-stage is thus defined recursively. At the first sub-stage, define $F_1 = \{(x_{A,2}, x_1) : x_{A,2} + x_1 = \Pi^C\}$ to be the feasible set. At the ith sub-stage, the feasible set, defined recursively, is $F_i = \{(x_{A,i+1}, x_i) : x_{A,i+1} + x_i = \Pi^C\}$. At the ith sub-stage, the ith bargaining game is constrained by the ith feasible set and is given by $\max_{(x_{A,i+1}, x_i) \in F_i} (x_{A,i+1})^\alpha (x_i)^\beta$. Thus, at the nth sub-stage, the bargaining problem reduces to $\max_{(x_A, x_n) \in F_n} (x_A)^\alpha (x_n)^\beta$, where x_A is the share of the channel profit that the assembler receives when negotiation with the nth supplier. Working backwards and solving constrained problems at each step, we can solve these recurrence relations to obtain the shares of Π^C for the assembler and suppliers. The following is the result of this process. The profit of the assembler and the ith supplier are respectively: $\pi_A = \alpha^n \Pi^C$ and $\pi_i = \alpha^{i-1} \beta \Pi^C$. The outcomes crucially depend on the order in which the negotiations are done. Notice that suppliers prefer to go earlier in the sequence and the assembler is indifferent. This is a weakness of this type of analysis. In an ideal setting, an axiomatic framework, if one exists, would remove such dependences. In this setting, one can resort to a sub-game where suppliers pay for favorable positions (this can be done in many ways, through a direct payment game or an auction). The equilibrium of such a sub-game smoothens the dependence on the sequence and yields all suppliers an equal payoff, but substantially increases the assembler's utility. This is once again an artifact of exogenously endowing the assembler with the power to choose sequences. A further criticism of such sequential negotiation games is that they are not immune from hold up issues. Several restrictive assumptions need to be made for this to work. The analysis assumes that once the assembler negotiates the terms of a contract with a supplier, they sign a conditional contract. The contingency in the contract is that the actual transaction will take place only if an agreement is reached with all suppliers. The reason for such an agreement is to prevent "hold up" problems which may arise. For instance, if the assembler pays suppliers as soon as each negotiation ends, the last supplier in the negotiation sequence can extract greater profits from the assembler who has already paid for the components from the previous $n - 1$ suppliers, but cannot assemble the final product without the components provided by the last supplier. An obvious remedy to many of the above problems is to simply assume that all players engage in an $N + 1$ Nash bargaining game. Note that, in this setting, this is not in the assembler's interest as he earns a higher utility by adopting a sequential approach.

2.9 Multi-Echelon Networks

We next turn our attention to multi-echelon network models similar to the ones studied by Corbett and Karmarkar [37] and Carr and Karmarkar [28] discussed in Section 1 and see how a bargaining approach may work in such situations. An important paper in bargaining in supply chain networks is Lovejoy [69] that looks at a bargaining solution for a multi-echelon serial type system with multiple players selling substitutes in some of the tiers. As with many of the above models, there does not exist a ready-made bargaining solution that can be applied to this situation. We first describe the setting and then the solution used in Lovejoy [69]. The following is from his work.

Consider a firm that designs a new product and wishes to bring it to market, but does not have ownership or control over all of the resources required to make that happen. Assume the product is sufficiently differentiated from current offerings in non-price attributes that the designing firm is, at least temporarily, a monopolist in the market. The firm must select and contract with one of several possible tier 1 suppliers for necessary inputs, who do the same with their (tier 2) suppliers, etc. In the tiers of the supply chain closer to the monopolist and the finished goods market the required inputs are product-specific and, due to fixed tooling and/or relationship costs, a single supplier in each tier will emerge as active. At some point moving upstream in the supply chain, the inputs become substitutable commodities and multiple suppliers may be active, delivering standardized inputs at market competitive prices. This general situation can be found in a range of industries including high tech, consumer products and services, family and entertainment, food, furniture, B-to-B services, automotive and large complex engineered products. Lovejoy analyzes the efficiency and distributional outcomes in such $m \times n$ supply chains (with m firms in tier 1 and n in tier 2) characterized by tier-wise negotiations, horizontal competition, sole-sourcing and complete local information. No solution concept yet exists in the literature for this context, yet it is a reasonable representation of many real supply chains. The assumption of sole sourcing is an important one in his work. A situation where this will arise is one where players sell perfectly substitutable goods/services in any tier. Nevertheless, even with sole sourcing, we do not have a bargaining solution that we can apply. Lovejoy uses a concept called the *balanced principal*. The balanced principal solution to an $m \times n$ supply chain bargaining problem predicts which two firms will emerge with the contract, and what the transfer price between them will be. The paper shows that the most efficient two firms will be the contracting pair because they can beat any other bid and remain profitable. Lovejoy also shows that the price prediction is an extension of classical bilateral bargaining theory, in that it collapses to the classical solution when the latter is applicable.

3

Future Research and Conclusions

This review started out with a description of models of supply-chain competition. We reviewed a collection of papers in the operations management literature addressing various models of vertical and horizontal competition, focusing on aspects of the models that help ensure the existence of an equilibrium. While our understanding of competitive interactions in single-stage or infinite-horizon settings is broad, additional work needs to be done in the context of multi-period dynamic competition and contracting.

The review also includes a discussion of supply-chain coordination, wherein the centralized solution is achieved by the implementation of a specifically designed coordinating contract. The alternative to supply-chain coordination involves an equilibrium solution in which the system's power structure, as given, for example, by the order of play, determines the relative performance of all parties in the supply chain. The coordinating contracts usually allow for an arbitrary allocation of supply-chain profit, so the question of how firms agree on a specific division of profit is of interest. This question lead to a discussion of bargaining models and the conceptualization of bargaining power. In particular, we review the Nash bargaining and Generalized Nash bargaining models, as well as other models of negotiation power.

Specifically, we first describe the Nash bargaining framework applied to a singe-seller single-buyer system. We show that this is a straightforward model as long as players are risk neutral. We then look at instances where at least one of the players is risk averse. We then describe some settings with multiple players in at least one of the tiers and demonstrate a few applications of Nash bargaining. We also mention many of the strong assumptions that are made. Finally, we discuss the balanced principal concept. We hope it is clear to the reader that extending the two party bilateral negotiation models to multiple players in a supply chain requires strong assumptions and is somewhat challenging.

Although we have described a few applications of cooperative bargaining to supply chain models, the field is still at its infancy. There are numerous issues that require the attention of the researchers. We mention a few that we feel are worth exploring in future research.

In our discussion on relative channel power, one of the issues we explored was risk-aversion and how it affects bargaining outcomes between players in a very specific setting. We discussed the effect of risk aversion in non-cooperative supply chain models as well. A few things that one may immediately notice from the discussions on this topic is the dependency of the results on the contract type that is being negotiated. That is, elegant approaches from industrial organization such as simple transfers or using a large set of contract parameters for achieving the optimal outcome may not simply suffice. At its heart, when players are risk averse, mechanisms that share risk genuinely come into the picture. This creates modeling and technical issues when trying to extend these types of discussions to multi-player systems (with more than two players). In the scope of bargaining games, although attitudes to risk is a primitive of Nash bargaining, we do not yet know how to extend our analysis to some of the above multi-tier systems to include risk-averse players. This is an area of research that could yield some significant insights.

Yet another aspect of modeling and understanding channel power and its effect is how one captures negotiation power effectively within the bargaining model without exogenous specifications. Note that our earlier discussion in Sections 1 and 2 used exogenous specifications such as reservation levels, risk aversion etc. We illustrate this issue by using a simple example. Consider two suppliers selling to a single retailer. Let us assume that the suppliers are selling partially substitutable products. The retailer buys from the two suppliers and decides its assortment (how much of each product to keep and possibly their prices). Further, let all players be risk neutral. This is similar to the model studied in Choi [34]. One can ask several interesting and practical questions based on this model setting. First, how does one design a bargaining game between the retailer and the two suppliers? From a practical perspective, it is unlawful for all three players to simultaneously negotiate cooperatively. Even if we set aside such restrictions, the Nash bargaining game, as such, directly applied, does not answer the question satisfactorily. For instance, solving the 3-player Nash bargaining game would lead to an allocation of a third of the efficient profit to each player. This outcome is not satisfactory for several reasons. First, this allocation does not reflect possible power structures. For instance, if the degree of substitution is asymmetric, one would expect the supplier with the more attractive product to get a higher share than the other supplier. Moreover, in the supply chain that we just described, the retailer, by virtue of having a pivotal role (that is, the retailer can align with one supplier and ignore the other, but the suppliers by themselves achieve no value) exerts a certain influence on the chain that the 3-person game, naively used, does not reflect. That is, an inherent model of demand that tracks this fact that one of the suppliers sells a more profitable product will be completely ignored by a typical bargaining solution such as the one by Nash. One can fix this by specifying bargaining powers exogenously, but this is unsatisfactory as one would expect a reasonable analysis to yield allocations according to the endogenous specifications of the model. Returning to the equal allocation, it suffers from another problem, i.e., it may not be coalition proof, namely, the retailer could simply pair up with one of the suppliers and not stock the other supplier's product rather than suffer a third of the share. To cast this in the scheme of cooperative games, one can use the aforementioned idea, the Core [48], a well-known concept in cooperative games. The Core tackles the following issue. Consider N players engaged in joint actions that create a certain surplus (payoff). Core is a solution concept that looks at how this surplus should be divided between the players so that the grand coalition which achieves the highest surplus is sustained. In other words, the core is the set of allocations under which no coalition has a value greater than the sum of its members' payoffs. Therefore, no coalition has incentive to leave the grand coalition and receive a larger payoff. In a two person bargaining game, the Nash bargaining solution trivially yields a core allocation as no player can defect and do better than the negotiated outcome. The balanced principal solution also achieves a core allocation for the serial system that it tackles. When seeking to devise a bargaining framework for problems such as the one in Choi [34], one needs to be acutely aware if the negotiated solution deters defections by sub-coalitions that comprise a subset of suppliers and the retailer. A part of the problem is because of how disagreement outcomes are modeled. Another is in part due to the fact that the Nash bargaining solution is symmetric. If we resort to the GNB game, one would hope that the indices in the objective function that represent relative power of the players can be endogenously derived using the primitives of the problem — the degree of substitution in this case. The industrial organization literature seems to have better answers to this setting, wherein a non-cooperative contracting game is played and the equilibrium contract is derived. This contract can be tweaked to be efficient. If we re-visit the analysis in Bernstein and Marx [18], we can see how one can use the endogenous reservation levels and suitable contracts to understand the effect of power in the supply chain. Note that, in a cooperative setting, the balanced principal cannot be applied to the problems discussed here. The balanced principal solution works only for the case when the products are perfectly substitutable. To do such an analysis using a cooperative bargaining framework seems to be an open problem worth pursuing.

References

[1] E. Adida and V. DeMiguel, "Supply chain competition with multiple manufacturers and retailers," *Operations Research*, vol. 59, no. 1, pp. 156–172, 2011.

[2] V. Agrawal and S. Seshadri, "Risk intermediation in supply chains," *IIE Transactions*, vol. 32, no. 9, pp. 819–831, 2000.

[3] N. Altintas, F. Erhun, and S. Tayur, "Quantity discounts under demand uncertainty," *Management Science*, vol. 54, no. 4, pp. 777–792, 2008.

[4] R. Anupindi and Y. Bassok, "Centralization of stocks: Retailers vs. manufacturer," *Management Science*, vol. 45, no. 2, February 1999.

[5] R. Anupindi and Y. Bassok, "Supply contracts with quantity commitments and stochastic demand," in *Quantitative Models of Supply Chain Management*, (S. Tayur, R. Ganeshan, and M. Magazine, eds.), Kluwer Academic Publishers, 1999.

[6] K. Arrow, "Aspects of the theory of risk bearing," in *Essays in the Theory of Risk Bearing*, Markham, Chicago, 1965.

[7] S. B. Bacharach and E. J. Lawler, *Bargaining, Power, Tactics and Outcomes*. Jossey-Bass, San Francisco, 1981.

[8] O. Baron, O. Berman, and D. Wu, "Bargaining within the supply chain and its implication to coordination of supply chains in an industry," Working Paper Rotman School of Business, University of Toronto, 2008.

[9] F. Bernstein and G. DeCroix, "Decentralized pricing and capacity decisions in a multitier system with modular assembly," *Management Science*, vol. 50, pp. 1293–1308, 2004.

[10] F. Bernstein and G. DeCroix, "Inventory policies in a decentralized assembly system," *Operations Research*, vol. 54, no. 2, pp. 324–336, 2006.

[11] F. Bernstein, G. DeCroix, and Y. Wang, "Incentives and commonality in a decentralized multi-product assembly system," *Operations Research*, vol. 55, pp. 630–646, 2007.

[12] F. Bernstein and A. Federgruen, "Pricing and replenishment strategies in a distribution system with competing retailers," *Operations Research*, vol. 51, no. 3, pp. 409–426, 2003.

[13] F. Bernstein and A. Federgruen, "A general equilibrium model for industries with price and service competition," *Operations Research*, vol. 52, no. 6, pp. 868–886, 2004.

[14] F. Bernstein and A. Federgruen, "Decentralized supply chains with competing retailers under demand uncertainty," *Management Science*, vol. 51, no. 1, pp. 18–29, 2005.

[15] F. Bernstein and A. Federgruen, "Coordination mechanisms for supply chains under price and service competition," *Manufacturing and Service Operations Management*, vol. 9, no. 3, pp. 242–262, 2007.

[16] F. Bernstein and G. Kök, "Dynamic cost reduction through process improvement in assembly networks," *Management Science*, vol. 55, no. 4, pp. 552–567, 2009.

[17] F. Bernstein, G. Kök, and A. Meca, "Cooperation in assembly systems: The role of knowledge sharing networks," Duke University Working Paper, 2011.

[18] F. Bernstein and L. Marx, "Reservation profit levels and the division of supply chain profit," Working Paper, Duke University, 2008.

[19] T. Boyaci, "Competitive stocking and coordination in a multiple-channel distribution system," *IIE Transactions*, vol. 37, pp. 407–427, 2005.

[20] G. Cachon, "Supply chain coordination with contracts," Chapter 6 in *Handbooks in Operations Research and Management Science: Supply Chain Management*, 2003.

[21] G. Cachon, "Stock wars: Inventory competition in a two-echelon supply chain with multiple retailers," *Operations Research*, vol. 49, no. 5, pp. 658–674, 2001.

[22] G. Cachon and M. Lariviere, "Capacity allocation using past sales: When to turn-and-earn," *Management Science*, vol. 45, no. 5, pp. 685–703, 1999.

[23] G. Cachon and M. Lariviere, "Supply chain coordination with revenue-sharing contracts: Strengths and limitations," *Management Science*, vol. 51, pp. 33–44, 2005.

[24] G. Cachon and S. Netessine, "Game theory in supply chain analysis," *INFORMS TutORials in Operations Research*, Paul Gray, Series Editor, pp. 200–233, 2006.

[25] G. Cachon and F. Zhang, "Obtaining fast service in a queuing system via performance-based allocation of demand," *Management Science*, vol. 53, no. 3, pp. 408–420, 2007.

[26] G. Cachon and P. Zipkin, "Competitive and cooperative inventory policies in a two-stage supply chain," *Management Science*, vol. 45, no. 7, pp. 936–953, 1999.

[27] F. Caro and V. Martinez-de-Albeniz, "The impact of quick response in inventory-based competition," *Manufacturing and Service Operations Management*, vol. 12, no. 3, pp. 409–429, 2010.

[28] S. Carr and U. Karmarkar, "Competition in multiechelon assembly supply chains," *Management Science*, vol. 51, no. 1, pp. 45–59, 2005.

[29] G. Caruana and L. Einav, "A theory of endogenous commitment," Working Paper, Stanford University, 2003.

[30] F. Chen, A. Federgruen, and Y.-S. Zheng, "Coordination mechanisms for a distribution system with one supplier and multiple retailers," *Management Science*, vol. 47, no. 5, pp. 693–708, 2001.

[31] X. Chen, S. Shum, and D. Simchi-Levi, "Coordinating and rational contracts in supply chains," Working Paper, M.I.T., 2010.

[32] S.-H. Cho, "Horizontal mergers in multi-tier decentralized supply chains," Working Paper, Carnegie Mellon University, 2011.

[33] J. Chod and N. Rudi, "Strategic investments, trading and pricing under forecast updating," *Management Science*, vol. 52, no. 12, pp. 1913–1929, December 2006.

[34] S. Choi, "Price competition in a channel structure with a common retailer," *Marketing Science*, vol. 10, pp. 271–296, 1991.

[35] T.-M. Choi, D. Li, and H. Yan, "Mean-variance analysis of a single supplier and retailer supply chain under a returns policy," *European Journal of Operational Research*, vol. 184, pp. 356–376, 2008.

[36] C. Corbett and X. de Groote, "A supplier's optimal quantity discount policy under asymmetric information," *Management Science*, vol. 46, no. 3, pp. 444–450, 2000.

[37] C. Corbett and U. Karmarkar, "Competition and structure in serial supply chains," *Management Science*, vol. 47, no. 7, pp. 966–78, 2001.

[38] C. Corbett and C. Tang, "Designing supply contracts: Contract type and information asymmetry," in *Quantitative Models of Supply Chain Management*, (S. Tayur, R. Ganeshan, and M. Magazine, eds.), Kluwer Academic Publishers, 1999.

[39] J. Cutcher-Gershenfeld, R. B. McKersie, and R. E. Walton, *Pathways to Change: Case Studies of Strategic Negotiations*. Kalamazoo, MI: W.E. Upjohn Institute for Employment Research, 1995.

[40] L. Dong and N. Rudi, "Who benefits from transshipment? Exogenous vs. endogenous wholesale prices," *Management Science*, vol. 50, no. 5, pp. 645–657, 2004.

[41] J. Eliashberg, "Arbitrating a dispute. A decision analytic approach," *Management Science*, vol. 32, pp. 963–974, 1986.

[42] H. Emmons and S. M. Gilbert, "Note: The role of returns policies in pricing and inventory decisions for catalogue goods," *Management Science*, vol. 44, no. 2, pp. 276–283, 1998.

[43] K. Ertogral and S. D. Wu, "A bargaining game for supply chain contracting," Working Paper, Lehigh University, 2001.

[44] X. Fang, K. So, and Y. Wang, "Component procurement strategies in decentralized assemble-to-order systems with time-dependent pricing," *Management Science*, vol. 54, no. 12, pp. 1997–2011, 2008.

[45] Q. Feng and L. X. Lu, "The strategic perils of low-cost outsourcing," Forthcoming in *Management Science*, 2011.

[46] X. Gan, S. Sethi, and H. Yan, "Coordination of a supply chain with risk-averse agents," *Production and Operations Management*, vol. 13, no. 2, pp. 135–149, 2004.

[47] Y. Gerchak and Y. Wang, "Revenue-sharing vs. wholessale-price contracts in assembly systems with random demand," *Production and Operations Management*, vol. 13, no. 1, pp. 23–33, 2004.

[48] D. B. Gillies, "Solutions to general non-zero sum games," in *Contributions to the Theory of Games IV*, (A. W. Tucker and R. D. Luce, eds.), pp. 47–83, Princeton University Press, 1959.

[49] D. Granot and S. Yin, "On the effectiveness of returns policies in the price-dependent newsvendor model," *Naval Research Logistics*, vol. 52, no. 8, pp. 765–779, 2005.

[50] H. Gurnani and Y. Gerchak, "Coordination in decentralized assembly systems with uncertain component yields," *European Journal of Operational Research*, vol. 176, no. 3, pp. 1559–1576, 2007.

[51] H. Gurnani and M. Shi, "A business to business bargaining model with supply uncertainty," to appear in *Management Science*, 2005.

[52] A. Ha, L. Li, and S.-M. Ng, "Price and delivery logistics competition in a supply chain," *Management Science*, vol. 49, no. 9, pp. 1139–1153, 2003.

[53] B. C. Hartman, M. Dror, and M. Shaked, "Cores of inventory centralization games," *Games and Economic Behavior*, vol. 31, pp. 26–49, 2000.

[54] T. Huh, G. Janakiraman, and M. Nagarajan, "Competitive multi-period inventory models with demand substitution," Working Paper, Sauder School of Business, U.B.C., 2010.

[55] E. Kalai and M. Smorodinsky, "Other solutions to Nash's bargaining problem," *Econometrica*, vol. 43, pp. 513–518, 1975.

[56] E. Kandel, "The right to return," *Journal of Law and Economics*, vol. 39, no. 1, pp. 329–356, April 1996.

[57] R. Kohli and H. Park, "A cooperative game theory model of quantity discounts," *Management Science*, vol. 35, pp. 693–707, 1989.

[58] D. Kostamis and E. Kemahlioglu-Ziya, "Optimal selling to asymmetric retailers," University of North Carolina at Chapel Hill Working Paper, 2011.

[59] D. Kreps, *Game Theory and Economic Modeling*. Oxford University Press, 1990.

[60] H. Krishnan and R. A. Winter, "Vertical control of price and inventory," *American Economic Review*, vol. 97, no. 5, pp. 1840–1857, 2007.

[61] H. Krishnan and R. A. Winter, "Inventory dynamics and supply chain coordination," *Management Science*, vol. 56, no. 1, pp. 141–147, 2010.

[62] M. Lariviere, "Supply chain contracting and coordination with stochastic demand," in *Quantitative Models of Supply Chain Management*, (S. Tayur, R. Ganeshan, and M. Magazine, eds.), Kluwer Academic Publishers, 1999.

[63] M. Lariviere, "A note on probability distributions with increasing generalized failure rates," *Operations Research*, vol. 54, no. 3, pp. 602–604, May–June 2006.

[64] M. Lariviere and E. L. Porteus, "Selling to the newsvendor: An analysis of price-only contracts," *Manufacturing and Service Operations Management*, vol. 3, no. 4, pp. 293–305, Fall 2001.

[65] Q. Li and A. Ha, "Reactive capacity and inventory competition under demand substitution," *IIE Transactions*, vol. 40, no. 8, pp. 707–717, 2008.

[66] X. Li and Q. Wang, "Coordination mechanisms of supply chain systems," *European Journal of Operational Research*, vol. 179, no. 1, pp. 1–16, 2007.

[67] S. Lippman and K. McCardle, "The competitive newsboy," *Operations Research*, vol. 45, no. 1, pp. 54–65, 1997.

[68] Y. Liu, M. Fry, and A. Raturi, "Retail price markup commitment in decentralized supply chains," *European Journal of Operational Research*, vol. 192, pp. 277–292, 2009.

[69] W. Lovejoy, "Bargaining chains," Forthcoming in *Management Science*, 2010.

[70] S. Mahajan and G. van Ryzin, "Stocking retail assortments under dynamic consumer substitution," *Operations Research*, vol. 49, no. 3, pp. 334–351, May–June 2001.

[71] P. Majumder and A. Srinivasan, "Leadership and competition in network supply chains," *Management Science*, vol. 54, no. 6, pp. 1189–1204, June 2008.

[72] L. Marx and G. Shaffer, "Exclusion with downstream bargaining power," Working Paper, Duke University, 2004.

[73] L. Marx and G. Shaffer, "Upfront Payments and Exclusion in Downstream Markets," Working Paper, Duke University, 2004.

[74] T. McGuire and R. Staelin, "An industry equilibrium analysis of downstream vertical integration," *Marketing Science*, vol. 2, no. 2, pp. 161–191, 1983.

[75] A. Meca, J. Timmer, I. Garcia-Jurado, and P. Borm, "Inventory games," *European Journal of Operational Research*, vol. 156, no. 1, pp. 127–139, 2004.

[76] C. Munson and M. Rosenblatt, "Theories and realities of quantity discounts: An exploratory study," *Production and Operations Management*, vol. 7, pp. 352–369, 1998.

[77] A. Muthoo, "A bargaining model based on the commitment tactic," *Journal of Economic Theory*, vol. 69, pp. 134–152, 1996.

[78] M. Nagarajan and Y. Bassok, "A bargaining framework in supply chains: The assembly problem," *Management Science*, vol. 54, no. 8, pp. 1482–1496, 2009.

[79] M. Nagarajan and G. Sosic, "Game theoretical analysis of cooperation among supply chain agents: Review and extensions," *European Journal of Operations Research*, vol. 187, 2008.

[80] J. F. Nash, "The bargaining game," *Econometrica*, vol. 18, pp. 155–162, 1950.

[81] J. F. Nash, "Noncooperative games," *Annals of Mathematics*, vol. 54, pp. 286–295, 1951.

[82] S. A. Neslin and L. Greenhalgh, "Nash's theory of cooperative games as a predictor of the outcomes of buyer-seller negotiations: An experiment in media purchasing," *Journal of Marketing Research*, pp. 368–379, November 1983.

[83] S. A. Neslin and L. Greenhalgh, "The ability of Nash's theory of cooperative games to predict the outcomes of buyer-seller negotiations: A dyad-level test," *Management Science*, vol. 32, no. 4, pp. 480–498, 1986.

[84] S. Netessine and N. Rudi, "Centralized and competitive inventory models with demand substitution," *Operations Research*, vol. 51, no. 2, pp. 329–335, March–April 2003.

[85] S. Netessine, N. Rudi, and Y. Wang, "Inventory competition and incentives to back-order," *IIE Transactions*, vol. 38, pp. 883–902, 2006.

[86] S. Netessine and F. Zhang, "Positive vs. negative externalities in inventory management: Implications for supply chain design," *Manufacturing and Service Operations Management*, vol. 7, no. 1, pp. 58–73, Winter 2005.

[87] R. Parker and R. Kapuscinski, "Managing a non-cooperative supply chain with limited capacity," Forthcoming in *Operations Research*, 2010.

[88] M. Parlar, "Game theoretic analysis of the substitutable product inventory problem with random demands," *Naval Research Logistics*, vol. 35, no. 3, pp. 397–409, 1988.

[89] B. A. Pasternack, "Optimal pricing and return policies for perishable commodities," *Marketing Science*, vol. 4, no. 2, pp. 166–176, 1985.

[90] G. Perakis and G. Roels, "The price of anarchy in supply chains: Quantifying the efficiency of price-only contracts," *Management Science*, vol. 53, no. 8, pp. 1249–1268, 2007.

[91] N. C. Petruzzi and M. Dada, "Pricing and the newsvendor problem: A review with extensions," *Operations Research*, vol. 47, no. 2, pp. 183–194, 1999.

[92] E. L. Plambeck and T. A. Taylor, "Implications of breach remedy and renegotiation design for innovation and capacity," *Management Science*, vol. 53, no. 12, pp. 1859–1872, 2007.

[93] E. L. Plambeck and T. A. Taylor, "Implications of renegotiation for optimal contract flexibility and investment," *Management Science*, vol. 53, no. 12, pp. 1872–1886, 2007.

[94] J. W. Pratt, "Risk aversion in the small and large," *Econometrica*, vol. 32, pp. 122–136, 1964.

[95] A. Roth, *Axiomatic Models in Bargaining*. Springer-Verlag, 1979.

[96] A. Roth, *Handbook of Experimental Economics*. Princeton, New Jersey: Princeton University Press, 1995.

[97] A. E. Roth and U. Rothblum, "Risk aversion and nash's solution for bargaining games with risky outcomes," *Econometrica*, vol. 50, pp. 639–647, 1982.

[98] A. Rubinstein, "Perfect equilibrium in a bargaining model," *Econometrica*, vol. 50, no. 1, pp. 97–110, 1982.

[99] N. Rudi, S. Kapur, and D. Pyke, "A two-location inventory model with transshipment and local decision making," *Management Science*, vol. 47, pp. 1668–1680, 2001.

[100] T. Schelling, *The Strategy of Conflict*. Harvard University Press, 1960.

[101] C. Shi, S. Yang, Y. Xia, and X. Zhao, "Inventory competition for newsvendors under the objective of profit satisficing," *European Journal of Operational Research*, vol. 215, no. 2, pp. 367–373, 2011.

[102] Y. Song, S. Ray, and S. Li, "Structural properties of Buy-Back contracts for price-setting newsvendors," *Manufacturing and Service Operations Management*, vol. 10, no. 1, pp. 1–18, 2008.

[103] J. Spengler, "Vertical integration and antitrust policy," *Journal of Political Economy*, vol. 4, no. 58, pp. 347–352, 1950.

[104] D. Spulber, "Risk sharing and inventories," *Journal of Economic Behavior and Organization*, vol. 6, no. 1, 1985.

[105] T. Taylor, "Supply chain coordination under channel rebates with sales effort effects," *Management Science*, vol. 48, no. 8, pp. 992–1007, 2002.

[106] B. Tomlin, "Capacity investments in supply chains: Sharing the gain rather than sharing the pain," *Manufacturing and Service Operations Management*, vol. 5, no. 4, pp. 317–333, Fall 2003.

[107] S. Viswanathan and Q. Wang, "Discount pricing decisions in distribution channels with price-sensitive demand," *European Journal of Operational Research*, vol. 149, no. 3, pp. 571–587, 2003.

[108] J. von Neumann and O. Morgenstern, *Theory of Games and Economic Behavior*. Princeton, New Jersey: Princeton University Press, 1944.

[109] Q. Wang and M. Parlar, "A three-person game theory model of the substitutable product inventory problem with random demands," *European Journal of Operational Research*, vol. 76, pp. 83–97, 1994.

[110] Y. Wang and Y. Gerchak, "Capacity games in assembly systems with uncertain demand," *Manufacturing and Service Operations Management*, vol. 5, no. 3, pp. 252–267, Summer 2003.

[111] Z. K. Weng, "Channel coordination and quantity discounts," *Management Science*, vol. 41, pp. 1509–1522, 1995.

[112] Z. K. Weng, "Modeling quantity discounts under general price-sensitive demand functions: Optimal policies and relationships," *European Journal of Operational Research*, vol. 86, pp. 300–314, 1995.

[113] X. Xu and W. J. Hopp, "A monopolistic and oligopolistic stochastic flow revenue management model," *Operations Research*, vol. 54, no. 6, pp. 1098–1109, November 2006.

[114] M. E. Yaari, "Some remarks of risk aversion and their use," *Journal of Economic Theory*, vol. 1, pp. 315–329, 1969.

[115] X. Zhao and D. R. Atkins, "Newsvendors under simultaneous price and inventory competition," *Manufacturing and Service Operations Management*, vol. 10, no. 3, pp. 539–546, Summer 2008.